HERE TO MAKE FRIENDS

HERE TO MAKE FRIENDS

How to Make Friends as an Adult

HOPE KELAHER, LCSW

ULYSSES PRESS

Published by:
Ulysses Press
P.O. Box 3440
Berkeley, CA 94703
www.ulyssespress.com

ISBN: 978-1-64604-004-9
Library of Congress Catalog Number: 2019951431

Printed in Canada by Marquis Book Printing
10 9 8 7 6 5 4 3 2 1

Acquisitions editor: Casie Vogel
Managing editor: Claire Chun
Project editor: Claire Sielaff
Editor: Renee Rutledge
Proofreader: Jessica Benner
Cover design: Malea Clark-Nicholson
Interior design: what!design @ whatweb.com
Production: Jake Flaherty

CONTENTS

CHAPTER 5
MAKING CONNECTIONS 164

CHAPTER 6
PLAYING THE DIGITAL FIELD 184

CHAPTER 7
THE ART OF PUTTING YOURSELF
OUT THERE 204

CHAPTER 8
MAINTAINING AND ELIMINATING
FRIENDSHIPS

INTRODUCTION

Making friends is hard. In fact, I think it is one of the hardest things to do—especially nowadays. Unlike finding a romantic relationship or even a casual hookup, which are at the tip of our fingers with dating apps, finding friends requires putting yourself out there without a date or a plan. There's no definitive end goal in friendships like there is in a romantic relationship. Maybe you meet a few interesting people at a bar or a party, but then you have to deal with the follow-through. Maybe they seemed funny at first, but you later realize that they are terribly boring. Maybe you are too adventurous? Maybe the two of you do click, but then they go their way and you yours. What if you are all in, but they are all out?

Friend-finding is like fishing. Casting out the line and, several reels and hooks in, waiting for a bite. It can be tiring. And let's not forget about those days when you don't catch anything at all. How frustrating!

These days we all seem to be casting wide nets hoping to catch fish—excuse me—find friends. Every day we're tallying and logging Snaps, Friends, and Insta likes, but then what? Who is actually looking up from their device and saying to themselves, "I am going to DM this person because I want to get to know them better"? Sure, this may happen every now and then, but we all know that sliding into DMs is more of a hookup thing than a friend-finding move. We are a society glued to our screens and our virtual friends, because it is far easier to get to "know" someone without really getting to *know* someone. I too am a culprit of this. On Facebook, I recently started following this girl who lives in my neighborhood and went to my high school. I think her brother even dated a relative of mine. I digress. Her feed comes up frequently. I know her name, her husband's name, her child's name, and even where she lives. Full disclosure: As I'm writing this, I'm realizing how creepy this sounds, especially since I have never had enough courage to approach this person in real life. BUT she's my Facebook friend! Please tell me that I am not alone here!

The fact is that we live in a very different age of friendship than our predecessors did. In our world, physical communities are smaller and more transient. We have more expansive online social networks but fewer people there for us at the drop of a hat. More of us are in the gig economy where we migrate from job to job and workplace to workplace. Maybe we work in a shared workspace or from home. The truth is that we have fewer real-life opportunities than our parents did to meet possible friends around the office watercooler. How can we not feel slightly nostalgic for the days when friendships of utility, pleasure, and commitment were easily fostered in the workplace?

The reality is that we all need friends, and good ones at that. This book is meant for the introvert who struggles to find the energy to get out there and meet people, the extrovert who has too many friends but not enough good ones, those who struggle with social anxiety, the person who has limited access to community, and the person struggling to bridge the gap between their many virtual friends and their real-life friends. With customized strategies for whichever type or types of person you are, this book offers reassurance that, while friend-finding is hard, it *can* be done!

As a relational and systemic therapist, I think about the relationships that individuals have with themselves on an intrapsychic level, and the relationships that they have within a variety of contexts. As a result, I often find myself working with young people who are dealing with multiple life-course transitions, such as graduating college, starting a new job, or moving to the Big Apple. Many seek my help because of two common struggles: feelings of loneliness and the longing for community. These individuals are often struck by how much effort it takes to find "their" people while simultaneously navigating feelings brought on by "adulting." Even people who are settled in their careers know how difficult it can be to balance long work hours and a social life. More young and middle-age adults are seeking assistance in overcoming other barriers to making friends, such as social anxiety disorder, depression, introversion, and social awkwardness. In fact, it's normal to struggle with making friends, especially at times in your life that are full of change or transition.

Adults who have had success in finding and making friends often struggle in maintaining these friendships while managing other responsibilities. I often hear clients joke that maybe they should take their friends into counseling to work out relationship challenges as they would with a lover, partner, sibling, or family member. The irony here is that friendship is at the core of so many kinds of relationships but appears to be the one relational topic neglected the most. A common misconception is that making and keeping friends is an EASY thing. The reality is that no relationship is easy! Friendships sustain us through heartbreaks, difficulties, happiness, and life's hardships, so it's important that we nurture them as much as we nurture our other kinds of relationships. When thinking about the dynamics of friendship, I'm reminded of the popular sitcom *The Golden Girls* and its catchy theme song, "Thank You for Being a Friend."

The sitcom, for those who are not familiar, focuses on the triumphs and challenges that four older women—who end up being roommates by happenstance—encounter together and how they persevere thanks to the strength of their friendship. It's not surprising that this sitcom received critical acclaim and several awards. In fact, almost all beloved sitcoms, from *Friends* to *How I Met Your Mother*, revolve around a core group of friends. They all speak to something that we as humans covet—to be seen and heard by others in the best and worst of times without judgment. Truthfully, friendship may be one of the most rewarding human experiences life has to offer.

The contents of this book—its guidance and strategies for finding and keeping close friendships—have deep meaning for me on a personal level. The close friendships in my life have provided me shelter, comfort, and companionship in some of my most difficult moments. My hope is to share with you some research on friendship and practical ways to find and sustain close, meaningful friendships as an adult. Throughout the book I share examples of those who have embarked on their friendship journey. Their names and any other identifying information have been changed to protect their identity. My hope is that, by the time you finish this book, you will view friendship in a new light and move into the right frame of mind for making new friends and nurturing your old friendships. For those who are more introverted, I offer strategies to increase your energy to maximize your friend-finding capacity. For those who suffer from social anxiety, I provide strategies to help you alleviate these difficult feelings and feel more confident in yourself as you meet new people. For those who always have plans with friends but no one to support you when the going gets tough, I will help you develop skills for creating more intimate relationships. If you are seeking new friends because of past unhealthy or toxic relationships, I will help you identify the indicators of both healthy and unhealthy friendships.

CHAPTER 1

UNDERSTANDING FRIENDSHIP IN ADULTHOOD

Over the past two decades, considerable research has come out supporting the idea that friendship is one of the most important components of a person's health, well-being, and happiness. And when you think about it, it makes sense! How good does it feel to have a meaningful catch-up chat, or pick right back up where you left off with an old friend, even if it's been years since you last met in person? How fun is it to laugh until your sides hurt over inside jokes or embarrassing stories with someone who has the same sense of humor as you do? It's an unbeatable feeling, and it's also healthy for you! Friendship and emotional connection with others have been found to be helpful in reducing the risk of mortality and shortening the duration of physical and mental illness, and may promote health by contributing to the release of endorphins.

Friends not only provide emotional and social support, but, from an evolutionary perspective, have also provided protection, practical support, and, in some cases, economic aid. While friendship can be found within different intimate relationships such as among family members or romantic relationships, it's important to differentiate a familial (kinship) friend from a friend. A friend, for the purposes of this book, is defined as an individual whom one knows and with whom one has a bond of emotional closeness and reciprocity (meaning the giving and taking in a relationship). Unlike kinship friendship, nonfamilial friendship is a choice and can end at any moment. As a result, there tends to be more energy involved in securing and maintaining nonfamilial relationships.

Quantity vs. Quality

For many, the next obvious question is: What's more important, the quantity of friends or the quality of friendships? Although research indicates that both the size of your social circles and quality of those relationships play an important role in your health and well-being, given the demands of today's adults, balancing the two is not always feasible. Interestingly, research by anthropologist and psychologist Robin Dunbar indicates that there is a maximum number of friends that an individual can maintain at any given point in time. In his research, Dunbar asserts that the human brain only has the cognitive capacity to hold onto 150 friendships at a time.[1] Not all of the 150 people are closely connected friends; some are categorized as casual acquaintances. The research indicates that, of those 150 people, approximately 50 are individuals whom you might have a dinner party with or see at a gathering of mutual friends. On average, a much smaller number, 15 or so, are individuals who are considered close friends—those you can go to for sympathy or confide in when needed. Lastly, Dunbar's numbers suggest that each of us will have (plus or minus) five individuals we would consider our best friends—those with whom we can confide our innermost secrets, desires, and challenges. There can be fluidity in this group of around five, as individuals may ebb in and out of the realm of best to close friends.

Even though networks of friendships have expanded through digital outlets like Facebook, Snapchat, Twitter, and Instagram, the one thing that remains constant is that the strength of long-standing relationships depends on face-to-face contact. Seeing someone in person fosters a shared connection that you can't get on social media. "Shares" and "likes" do not equate to the same positive shared human experiences, as face-to-face greetings,

---

1 R.I.M. Dunbar, "The Anatomy of Friendship," *Trends in Cognitive Sciences* (January 2018): 32–51.

shared meals, or laughter. These shared human experiences are more likely to release endorphins—hormones that are related to pleasure, stress reduction, and the social bonding experience. Research shows that despite the ease of logging and documenting one's friendships on social media, virtual relationships are not a good enough replacement for real-life friendships.[2] The best explanation is that meaningful relationships still take time and that time spent connecting with virtual friends diminishes the time and energy available for nurturing relationships in person.

Dimensions of a Quality Friendship

Knowing that humans have a limited capacity for the number of friends may be reassuring for some, especially for those whose hobby it is to collect social media friends. But it raises the question of whether or not your friendships are good enough or of high quality. For many, the answer to such a complicated question is subjective. According to most writers on friendship, high-quality relationships are characterized by high levels of reciprocal helping behaviors, interdependence, emotional intimacy, and constructive conflict resolution.

---

2   Bruno Gonçalves, Nicola Perra, and Alessandro Vespignani, "Modeling Users' Activity on Twitter Networks: Validation of Dunbar's Number," *PLoS ONE* 6, no. 8 (2011): e22656, doi:10.1371/journal.pone.0022656.

Reciprocity

However, newer research suggests that there are multiple dimensions and indicators of quality friendships. High-quality friendships in both childhood and adulthood are marked by themes of complimentary reciprocity, meaning that good friends will often praise each other's successes, provide encouragement after failures, and help support each person's sense of self-esteem.[3]

Interdependence

Another dimension of quality friendship is the notion of interdependence. That similarity between two individuals creates coordination within the friendship, allowing the pair to gain more pleasure and rewards from the relationship. Even if each person is getting something different, what they receive from the friendship is equally as helpful as what the other person receives. For example, Jan may rely on Kit for relationship support while Kit relies on Jan for help with familial support.

Emotional Intimacy

The third most prominent and researched dimension in quality friendships is emotional intimacy, meaning that there is positive communication and mutual disclosures in the relationship. Research on quality childhood friendships

---

3   Thomas J. Berndt, "Friendship Quality and Social Development," *Current Directions in Psychological Science* 11, no. 1 (2002): 7-10, doi:10.1111/1467-8721.00157.

found that those children who identified having high levels of intimacy in their relationships also identified their friendship as being high in other positive features, suggesting that intimacy may be the most important factor in a high-quality relationship.[4]

Conflict Resolution

No friendship is perfect. Since even the best friendships have negative features, it's also important to explore conflict management within high-quality relationships and how this might even contribute to the quality of the overall friendship. While most high-quality friendships exhibit minimal levels of conflict, they are not entirely conflict-free. In fact, it would be concerning and even to a relationship's detriment if it were entirely conflict-free. Conflict and its healthy resolution can allow for more intimacy and greater connectivity in any relationship, especially a friendship. Think about a time when you and a friend had a disagreement. You likely experienced some anxiety and trepidation when you contemplated how you were going to address the issue, but when you took the risk and did it, you likely felt a sense of relief and resolve.

For instance, imagine one of your closest friends sends you a text and you are not sure of the tone. It seems unlike your friend to speak to you in this way, and you just know

---

4 Berndt, "Friendship Quality and Social Development."

that something is wrong. Perhaps you sense that they are mad at you. Though you are anxious about escalating the situation, you take a huge step to ask them what is going on and to tell them that you are concerned. They share that they were disappointed in something you did or said. Although the conflict or your behaviors are not resolved, the tension that was bubbling below the surface is now fair game for an open discussion. You both now know each other's perspectives and feelings. Now you both can breathe easy and move onto solving the issue. Research on conflict within adolescent relationships suggests that, as we age, conflict resolution changes from coercive problem-solving to constructive problem-solving.[5] In fact, in adolescence, the development of empathy—the ability to understand another's emotional state—helps friends better understand each other's feelings and perspectives.

Let's examine what conflict resolution might look like in a high-quality friendship. Shay and Jen have plans, but Shay worked late the night before and isn't feeling well. Shay knows that these plans are very important to Jen, but she really doesn't have enough energy or motivation to go out. Shay communicates to Jen how she is very tired and how she is worried that if she doesn't go, she will disappoint her. Jen, although disappointed, tells Shay that she

---

5   Minet De Wied, Susan J. T. Branje, and Wim H. J. Meeus, "Empathy and Conflict Resolution in Friendship Relations among Adolescents," *Aggressive Behavior* 33, no. 1 (2006), doi:10.1002/ab.20166.

understands and that they will be sure to see one another at a different time. Jen does not hold this against Shay, and their friendship recovers and continues to evolve. Without empathy, the conflict resolution in this scenario may have been very different, and the outcome may have left each person feeling unheard, unseen, and uncared for. We can see that both sides were able to openly, safely, and constructively have a conversation with the other friend, and the relationship grew stronger thanks to the resolution.

Based on what you've learned up until now, I hope you're starting to realize that it is not the quantity but the quality of friendships that matters. People typically have approximately five people they are closest to, 15 who orbit those close friends, 50 they know socially and would be comfortable socializing with at a party, and approximately 150 acquaintances. To have the most meaningful friendships and connections with others, try not to focus on expanding your outermost network of friends, but instead invest time and energy in your closest social circles. It's also important to note that your closest friends may at different times in your life move in and out of the different circles. For instance, perhaps a close friend from college is no longer part of your inner circle when you move to a new city, but remains within those 15 close friendships. It's natural for friendships to sometimes shift between circles like this and, who knows, if that friend moves to the same city as you, they could easily move back into your inner circle.

Quantity of Friendships

This exercise will help you to identify the quantity of your existing friendships. With you at the center of the circles, list the people who are your closest friends, closer friends, and a few in the outer two rings.

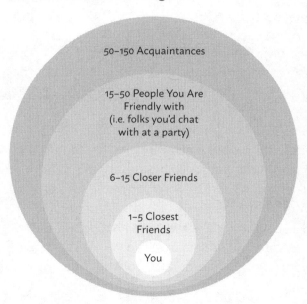

50–150 Acquaintances

15–50 People You Are
Friendly with
(i.e. folks you'd chat
with at a party)

6–15 Closer Friends

1–5 Closest
Friends

You

Now that you've identified the existing number of friendships within your circles, let's assess their quality. Consider the important dimensions of a quality friendship: reciprocity, interdependence, emotional intimacy, and conflict resolution. Examples of these dimensions as they exist within friendships are listed below:

Reciprocity

- Your friend is a good listener. They do not interrupt you when you are speaking and remain tuned in.

- They validate your concerns and worries, and there is equal back and forth.

- They are there for you when you need them the most and vice versa.

- They motivate you when you need encouragement, and you do this for them.

- Your friend knows when you are stressed and how to help without even asking.

Interdependence

- Your friend gives you space when you need it, and doing so is a non-issue.

- Your friend helps you reach your goals. Need a workout buddy, a plus one to that wedding, or a reminder that you are saving so you shouldn't buy that pair of jeans? They have your back.

- Your friend is reliable. They respect your boundaries and are there when you need them the most.

Emotional Intimacy

- You can be real with them and tell them the good, the bad, and the ugly—and they won't judge.

- You can trust them with your secrets.

- You can be your authentic self with them ALL the time.

- They know your hopes, dreams, and fears.

Conflict Resolution

- They can empathize with your situation and can see things from not only their perspective but yours as well.

- They forgive your misgivings and can address any concerns they have with you in a constructive way so that it does not derail your friendship.

- You both try not to take things too personally when either one of you is having a bad day.

- Feedback is collaborative and transparent.

Personal Self-Assessment

Using the above characteristics of quality friendships, take a personal self-assessment. Remember that to be in high-quality friendships you too must be a high-quality friend. Rate yourself as a friend on a scale of 1–10, with 10 being the highest, in each of these dimensions:

Your name:
Reciprocity:
Interdependence:
Emotional intimacy:
Conflict resolution:

Take note of the dimensions where your own contributions need some improvement.

Now, assess the quality of your closest friendships on the same scale of 1–10. Start with those friends in your inner-most circle, then assess the friend group within your second circle.

Friend's name:	Friend's name:
Reciprocity:	Reciprocity:
Interdependence:	Interdependence:
Emotional intimacy:	Emotional intimacy:
Conflict resolution:	Conflict resolution:

Friend's name:	Friend's name:
Reciprocity:	Reciprocity:
Interdependence:	Interdependence:
Emotional intimacy:	Emotional intimacy:
Conflict resolution:	Conflict resolution:

Friend's name:	Friend's name:
Reciprocity:	Reciprocity:
Interdependence:	Interdependence:
Emotional intimacy:	Emotional intimacy:
Conflict resolution:	Conflict resolution:

Friend's name:	Friend's name:
Reciprocity:	Reciprocity:
Interdependence:	Interdependence:
Emotional intimacy:	Emotional intimacy:
Conflict resolution:	Conflict resolution:

Friend's name:	Friend's name:
Reciprocity:	Reciprocity:
Interdependence:	Interdependence:
Emotional intimacy:	Emotional intimacy:
Conflict resolution:	Conflict resolution:

Friend's name:	Friend's name:
Reciprocity:	Reciprocity:
Interdependence:	Interdependence:
Emotional intimacy:	Emotional intimacy:
Conflict resolution:	Conflict resolution:

Take note of those friendships that are the strongest and weakest. Compare and contrast with your self-assessment.

Types of Friendships

Now that you have identified those individuals in your inner- and outermost circles, the quality of those relationships, and the way you contribute to positive friendships, you need to get a better understanding of the types of friendships you have. Why do some people land in your outermost circle versus your innermost circle? Could you even imagine the possibility of someone in your outermost circle—a distant acquaintance—becoming a close friend? What are the constructs of or barriers to such fluidity? What specifically makes some relationships stronger or weaker than others?

When trying to answer these larger questions, many turn to Aristotle, the ancient Greek philosopher. There's a reason why his thoughts and ideas have resonated with people across thousands of years! Aristotle's Nicomachean Ethics books explore his philosophy on how people can live their best lives. Not surprisingly, Aristotle devotes 2 out of these 10 books on the topic of friendship and how it is key to his notion of the "good life." Aristotle holds that friendship can only exist where there is mutual good between two people.[6] He then puts forth the three motivations for love and friendship: utility, pleasure, and goodness. Let's break down

---

6   Jason Ader, *Friendship in Aristotle's Nicomachean Ethics*, report, Parkland College, 2011, https://spark.parkland.edu/cgi/viewcontent.cgi?article=1038&context=ah.

these three motivations and see how they can apply to our lives.

Friendships of Utility

Friendships of utility are those relationships where both you and the other person benefit from it or find it useful (the expression "quid pro quo" comes to mind). You're in a friendship of utility for personal gain, not pleasure, and all friendly interactions must be mutually profitable. You're not hanging out just to hang out in a friendship of utility. As a result, these relationships can be rather weak, and the friendship bond is often superficial. Friendships of utility may serve a purpose, but their purpose is not companionship. Take, for example, a person who makes plans with someone for the weekend, but then cancels when better plans come along. In this scenario, there appears to be the initial, mutual goal of spending time together, but since the friendship is mainly superficial, the person doesn't consider the other's feelings when deciding to cancel. It's solely for their own benefit.

These types of relationships are common among acquaintances and are often developed when you're trying to make new friends. Perhaps the best and most common example of a utility friendship is one you establish when starting a new school or job, or when you're in an unfamiliar setting. For the sake of having something to do on a Friday night, have you ever found yourself going to a party where you didn't know anyone? Or sitting with the cool kids in the cafeteria for perceived social status, or maybe even befriending that girl in your gym class just so you have someone to talk to instead of standing around awkwardly? If so, then you have engaged in friendships of utility. Though not the most meaningful, these types of friendships can be useful, which is why all of us have and continue to engage in them.

Friendships of Pleasure

The second type of friendship is entirely based upon feeling good: pleasure friendships. The purpose of these types of relationships is for the individual to pursue what is pleasurable for themselves. You can typically find these sorts of friends in the third ring of your social circle. Perhaps they are those 50 or so friends that you might see at a party or public event. They are closer than acquaintances but not quite close enough to be within your more intimate circles. Consider people in college you spent time with because they were funny, entertaining, or adventurous. You might have felt an instant attraction or magnetism that pulled you toward them. While pleasure-seeking friendships have innate similarities, Aristotle likens them to "young" friendships because one's sense of pleasure changes over time. As a result, these friendships are likely to be short-term. Like the beginning phases of love where the romance feels to be all-encompassing and energizing, pleasure-based friendships often feel amazing at first. Yet they can also cool off as time passes because of their lack of depth.

Despite the possibility that pleasure-based relationships may not last, they are important in not only passing the time, but also in developing a sense of self. Through these relationships we learn about what and whom we like and dislike, and are given an opportunity to explore emotional intimacy with people. Consider a sports team you may have been on, work happy hours, or those with whom you play video games. They are positive, good-in-the-moment relationships that you mainly engage with around that specific activity. While some may evolve, most will taper off when either you or the other person is no longer interested in that activity. However, I would argue that we can and likely should have some of these types of relationships throughout our lives.

Friendships of the Good

The jackpot of all friendships is what Aristotle referred to as the "friendship of the good." Friendships of the good are based upon mutual admiration and love for one another. While they can include aspects of a pleasure friendship, or at least that is the ideal, these folks are your true comrades. They have your backs. There is complete reciprocity and openness. They will tell you the truth about yourself and have no shame and will still love and care for you, and you for them. In my experience these are the friends that you can call at time, for any reason, to vent about something at work or to mend a heartbreak. These friends are those who never let you lose focus of your true self. They light a fire when you need motivation or calm the flames when you are in danger of burning the house down. For many, "soul mate" or "best friend" are the terms used for friendships of the good.

You can see examples of platonic soul mates and best friends in countless movies and TV shows. Think the cast of *Entourage, Thelma and Louise*, or Bridget, Lena, Tibby, and Carmen of *The Sisterhood of the Traveling Pants*. I am personally reminded of *Beaches,* starring Bette Midler. The film is about two girls—a brunette and a redhead—from two very different walks of life who have nothing in common. But fate brings them together, and their relationship just sticks. These girls grow up to be teens, young adults, and middle-aged women who continue to have very little in common but are nonetheless connected. In one of the most poignant and meaningful scenes, we see the pure, platonic love they have for each other as they come to terms with the fact that one of them is dying.

These friendships aren't always gushy or full of melodramatic feelings, but they are easy. They help us grow. And they stay around far longer than any of the other types of friendship we've previously discussed.

Your Friendship Map

For this exercise, consider all of your friends within the first three innermost circles. Regardless of the type of friendship (utility, pleasure, or good) you may have with them, map them out using the image on page 27. Place yourself in the center and fill in the circles with your friends' names. Add more lines for more friends if needed. Once you have listed the names of your friends, try to identify if they are friends of utility, pleasure, or good.

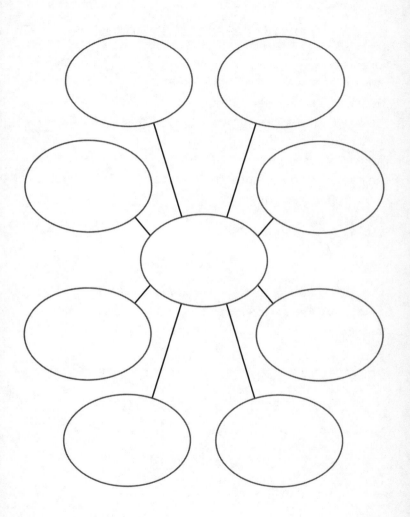

FRIENDS OF UTILITY	FRIENDS OF PLEASURE	BEST FRIENDS OR "PLATONIC SOUL MATES"

Consider if you'd like to further develop any of these friendships. Are there some relationships that don't seem to be as helpful as others? Why and why not?

_____

_____

_____

_____

_____

_____

List the friendships that you'd like to develop more. Then, next to the friend's name, describe what about that friendship you value.

_____

_____

_____

_____

_____

What You Value in Friendship

Since friendships are multidimensional, we each have personal preferences for what is most important in friendships and the types of friendships we value the most. Some people may prefer closely connected relationships, or those where they can confide their innermost secrets. Others may prefer friendships that are reliable, or relationships that bring adventure or pleasure. Knowing what you value the most and the least is important and useful in helping you develop your friend network and strengthen those existing relationships.

In the following spaces, evaluate five existing friendships for what needs development and what you value.

FRIENDSHIPS IN NEED OF DEVELOPMENT	WHAT YOU VALUE IN THAT FRIENDSHIP
1.	
2.	
3.	
4.	
5.	

List the top three qualities you value the most in your existing friendships.

1. _____

2. _____

3. _____

HERE TO MAKE FRIENDS

Summary

There are three primary types of friendships—friendships of utility, pleasure, and the good. Often, when we are first getting to know new people, we are likely to engage in friendships of utility, considering how this person may be helpful to us. Perhaps this person may be a good potential work contact or they set us up with a potential love interest. There is an obvious reason why we are engaged with this person. Many times, friendships of utility can and will evolve into friendships of pleasure. Consider that guy in the office whose desk is close to the CEO's door. While initially you might have worked up a cordial workplace friendship with him to get the first scoop on news coming out of the CEO's office (friendship of utility), over time you may realize that he's really cool, and maybe you would want to shoot hoops with him sometime (burgeoning pleasure relationship).

Say, over time, you two are still friends even though you 1) no longer work in the same place and 2) only occasionally shoot hoops, but develop a more intimate friendship, where maybe you both can express your hopes, dreams, and fears. If that's the case, then we have witnessed how a friendship of utility can evolve over time to a friendship of pleasure and then eventually a friendship of the good.

Friendships of utility and pleasure are ones where there needs to be reciprocity for them to last. As people change, so does their investment in friendships of utility and pleasure, whereas friendships of the good can often withstand varying levels of investment because there is already that deep, meaningful connection. Have you ever heard people say, "Even though we haven't talked in the longest time, it feels like we can just pick up where we started?" This denotes a friendship of the good.

While it may seem the optimal type of friendship is the "friendship of the good," that is not necessarily true. We need all three types of friendships to sustain our happiness. The more identities a person has, the more connections or friends they will have in the long term. For instance, if you embody multiple roles in your life, such as an employee, a volunteer, a soccer player, a gamer, and a hiker, then you will have more opportunities to connect with people. Multiple friendships of pleasure, whether they are long-lasting or not, are protective and can provide outlets for those bleak moments. Best friends, aka Aristotle's "friendships of the good," are those people with whom you experience pleasure and happiness. They feel like family members—family members we get to choose.

Think back to some of your past friendships. Did they fall into any of these categories? Do you miss any of those past friendships? If so, why? These relationships are obviously important, since we are interdependent creatures.

CHAPTER 2

FRIEND-FINDING: THEN AND NOW

"Hi, my name is (insert your name here). Will you be my friend?" If only making friends were that easy! Unfortunately, as we all know, it can be very hard. And, as you get older, finding and making friends becomes harder. I bet no one ever told you that acquiring and maintaining friends as an adult would take work. In fact, as a child, I thought that finding friends as an adult would be easier, that as an adult I would have free will to be my own person and meet people of my liking. In theory this is true, but few consider what it would be like to find friends without cultural institutions like school, work, and family to help.

Friendship in Early Childhood

For many of us, friend-finding started when we were small. Perhaps our parents took us to music classes, the park, or to day care. In these environments, we were placed with other children who, like us, had underdeveloped personalities. We learned how to share, navigate nuances of attention seeking and receiving, and move through our world. Exposure to such environments helped us build a sense of self and self-esteem that made us who we are today.

Many of our first friends are kinship friends, based on family connection. Siblings, cousins, and other relatives are often the first people we meet as we start our journey toward socialization. These are people whom our parents chose for us because of ease, commonality, or proximity. In early childhood, friendships are often characterized by and organized through playdates. Again, these relationships are not likely of our choosing, are dependent on age, and are heavily monitored by parents or caregivers. That said, any conflict that arises is typically addressed and resolved by parents. These earliest relationships are contingent on play and imagination. Children who demonstrate a degree of openness and friendliness are most successful at making friends. Children who are shier than others may struggle in play, which is a precursor to friendship.

As we enter social institutions such as elementary school, we become more autonomous in our ability to pick and choose possible friends. Many people assume that similarity breeds friendship, but this is true only to a certain extent. For instance, two children may be from the same neighborhood, ride the same school bus, and even be in the same class, but not be friends. That said, we know that children, like adults, tend to gravitate toward others who are like them. For instance, consider those school cliques we all encountered during our youth. Children who enjoyed the same interests, had similar home environments, and even had similar life experiences, such as having an older or younger sibling, tended to gravitate toward one another.

A key factor in early childhood friendships is fun. As with those pleasure friendships found in adulthood, shared fun in childhood is critical for the sustainability of the relationship. Remember those playdates from childhood when the opening question and response were likely, *"Hi! What do you want to do?"* *"I don't know, what do you want to do?"* Early childhood research on friendship looked at the development of friendship among unacquainted children and learned that the children who were best suited for one another were those who were able to sustain a shared activity during their playdates.

All in all, it is obvious why making and settling into friendships as young children is easier than making friends as we get older. Friendships at that age were essentially based on three components: proximity, similarity, and fun. These friendships, and even the activities in which we engaged in, were likely organized by our parents/caregivers—we had little skin in the game at this point. If someone didn't like us, we could likely move around and try to find *someone else* who was more open, more similar, and more fun.

First Friendships

This exercise is meant to help you reflect on your very first friendships. Think back to when you were 10 years old and younger. With whom did you have playdates? How long were those relationships? Are you friends with any of those people now? Create your list below.

PLAYDATE FRIENDS	LENGTH OF RELATIONSHIP	FRIENDS NOW? (Y/N)

Friendship in Middle School: Preteen Friendships

Making friends and keeping them becomes a higher-stakes game as children move on from elementary school. Friendships during this period mean everything. The making and breaking of friendships can feel like life or death for many preteens. At this age, friendships not only help you have a sense of identity, but also signify who you are to others. The notion of the clique becomes of utmost importance. Are you a jock? Are you into Comic-Con? Are you on student council? Or are you obsessed with video games?

During your preteen years, you don't entirely know yourself. At this stage of life, you are focused on getting a sense of who you are vis-à -vis other people. Perhaps you test-drive one social group one day and another the next. You are not quite affiliated with one group of people. This is common, and it is critical to one's self development. One day you might like soccer, the next day backgammon. Preteens are like chameleons—constantly changing their colors until something fits. This is a period of flexibility. You likely associated yourself with peer groups where there was both similarity and pleasure. The development of intimacy among peers begins. Who can keep that secret and who can't? Preteens are assessing who is trustworthy and who isn't—essentially determining who can be their close intimates or the friends of the good.

Research indicates that our need for friendship orientation, or collecting and cultivating friendship, peaks in mid-adolescence during the same period when friends appear to have large influence on one's overall well-being.[7] For instance, during this period of our development, supportive friendships can aid in motivation and mitigate identity problems. The friends that we associate with during this stage of our development serve as role models for social norms as well as positive and negative behaviors.

Friendship attraction during early adolescence resembles friendship attraction in early childhood, with a couple of key exceptions. Preteens are attracted to those who are like them, who are close in proximity to them, and with whom they can have fun. During early adolescence, however, gender preferences start to organize relationships and preteens have more autonomy over the friends they choose. Research indicates that female friendship circles during this period tend to be smaller and more intimate. Girls appear to prefer relationships that focus on disclosure and closeness, and boys focus on shared activities and status.[8] At this time in your life you might want to text, chat, or hang out with your friends incessantly.

7 Robert Crosnoe, "Friendships in Childhood and Adolescence: The Life Course and New Directions," Social *Psychology Quarterly* 63, no. 4 (2000): 377-391, doi:10.2307/2695847.

8 Crosnoe, "Friendships in Childhood and Adolescence."

Early-Adolescent Friendships

Identify whom you were closest to during your early adolescence. Where are these people now? Would you be interested in connecting with them? What were the social institutions (e.g., school, religious community, after-school settings) that brought you together?

TOP 5 FRIENDS DURING EARLY ADOLESCENCE	FRIENDS NOW? (Y/N)
1.	
2.	
3.	
4.	
5.	

Where did you meet these top 5 friends of your preteens?

_____

_____

_____

Friendship in High School: The Teenage Years

Having friends in middle school and as one moves into high school is important for some clearly obvious and some not-so-obvious reasons. New research indicates that close friendships in middle and high school have long-term positive impact on mental health.[9] In fact, the same research found a correlation between high-quality friendships (characterized by attachment, support, and directness) and reduced symptoms of depression and anxiety. Those teens who made a priority of developing close relationships during high school were found to have less social anxiety and higher self-esteem by age 25 compared to others. Those kids who were perceived to be popular in high school were found to have more social anxiety and depressive symptomology than those who cultivated close friendships. It seems being well-liked by many people is not as beneficial as having quality, intimate friendships.

For some, this research may bring a sigh of relief, especially if you were like me and not cool in high school. But it also raises some concerns for those of us who were exposed to social media platforms in high school and as we entered college. For us, our high school friends were often made

9   Rachel K. Narr et al., "Close Friendship Strength and Broader Peer Group Desirability as Differential Predictors of Adult Mental Health," *Child Development* 90, no. 1 (2017): 298–313, doi:10.1111/cdev.12905.

HERE TO MAKE FRIENDS

via social networking as we moved up through the grades, which means we can oftentimes have more superficial friendships than meaningful ones from that time period onward.

I probably don't need to remind you of how challenging it was to make friends in person when first entering high school! The transition into high school means making new friends, possibly shedding the old ones, and learning new social codes. Unlike middle school, the stakes in high school are higher, as there is not only social but also academic pressure. That's why it's so important to have supportive friends in high school. Research indicates that a key protective factor during this stage is having friends who are going through a similar type of transition.[10]

Middle school was where friendships were primarily based upon proximity, similarity, and pleasure/fun. As you move into high school, you mature and develop new likes and dislikes that perhaps you didn't have in middle school. We've learned that similarity and what brings people pleasure changes over time, resulting in the risk of some middle school friendships ending. This makes sense, as the differences between friends as they enter high school become more pronounced and often result in the friendship ending. A study completed by Florida

10   Berndt et al., "Influences of Friends and Friendships on Adjustment to Junior High School," *Merrill-Palmer Quarterly*, November 30, 1998, accessed May 09, 2019, https://eric.ed.gov/?id=EJ582404.

Atlantic University that tracked 410 seventh graders and checked in with them until senior year of high school indicated that only one pair of them remained friends.[11] From this study we can see how there is actually a very low probability that you will remain friends with those people you were close to in seventh grade.

In many ways, this idea makes perfect sense. The need for peer affiliations and to fit in becomes more pronounced in high school. Maybe your eighth-grade bestie takes up robotics while you join the track team. While you might occasionally share some good times, it just seems to make more sense to hang with people more like you. Relationships in high school serve as a microcosm for how you will be received in the world when you are an adult. We all know that there's almost nothing worse than having to chat with someone with whom you have nothing in common!

Nonetheless, those friendships gained and discarded in the later teenage years are unique and important as they not only help us identify who we are to the outside world, but also help us navigate other relational needs, such as romantic relationships. While, for some, this may have started during early adolescence, in high school, friends serve as an important gateway for dating opportunities.

---

11   Amy C. Hartl, Brett Laursen, and Antonius H. N. Cillessen, "A Survival Analysis of Adolescent Friendships: The Downside of Dissimilarity," *Psychological Science*, August 2015, accessed July 08, 2019, https://www.ncbi.nlm.nih.gov/pmc/articles/PMC4529362.

Think back to high school and how many couples were introduced through mutual friends. Remember telling a friend about a crush and hoping your crush would somehow hear about it? Or when you unexpectedly became available and needed a hookup or a rebound? Lastly, let's not forget when you got your heart broken and needed someone by your side—who was there to help?

Moreover, friendship during late adolescence and early adulthood is especially unique because you can function in a more autonomous manner. You are given more freedom in your last few years of high school, and you can experiment—remember the unsupervised house party? That said, high school friends are there for you when you come of age, and the history that you have with them will create bonds unlike other friendships that you have as an adult. High school friends bear witness to so many of your struggles—those interpersonal battles with your parents and siblings, your highs and lows, your failures, your successes. Unlike other friends, your high school friends have, to some degree, access to your entire life. It's like that scene from *Friday Night Lights* where the high schoolers know the details of Tim Riggin's family life and the fact that Matt Saracen has to take care of his grandmother. I digress. My point is that few people in your life will have the opportunity to *really know you,* and the reality is that it's often those high school friends.

Another important feature of high school friendships is the prevalence of platonic male-female friendships. While there isn't a plethora of research in this area, the research notes two important things:[12]

1. Female relationships from middle school to high school are rather unstable.

2. Male friendships during this developmental state are rather stable.

Because teenage girls place a greater value on intimacy, closeness, and trustworthiness, when any one of these values is violated, the relationship is at risk of ending. Teenage boys do value the same things, but appear to value companionship over everything else.[13] This research hypothesizes that since boys tend to be easier going and more accepting of relationship challenges in friendships than their female counterparts, they experience fewer ruptures. Another possible reason is that, as boys age and succumb to the many gender stereotypes about masculinity, they do not feel comfortable expressing their emotions when a rupture does occur and, as a result, do not share their feelings with others. Later in the book, we

12 Joyce F. Benenson and Athena Christakos, "The Greater Fragility of Females versus Males Closest Same-Sex Friendships," *Child Development* 74, no. 4 (2003) , doi:10.1111/1467-8624.00596.

13 Jeffrey A. Hall, "Sex Differences in Friendship Expectations: A Meta-analysis," *Journal of Social and Personal Relationships* 28, no. 6 (2010): 723, doi:10.1177/0265407510386192.

HERE TO MAKE FRIENDS

will discuss the role vulnerability plays in developing and maintaining friendships.

Identify Your Closest High School Friends

Now that we have explored the developmental process of making friends from early childhood to late adolescence, identify who you were closest to in high school. Ask yourself: Are you still close with these people? If you aren't, could you imagine reconnecting with them? Ask yourself why you were friends with them in the first place.

TOP 5 FRIENDS DURING HIGH SCHOOL	ARE YOU FRIENDS NOW? (Y/N)	COULD YOU IMAGINE RECONNECTING? (Y/N)
1.		
2.		
3.		
4.		
5.		

Where did you meet these top 5 high school friends?

1. _____

_____

2. _____

_____

3. _____

_____

4. _____

_____

5. _____

_____

HERE TO MAKE FRIENDS

Who Considered You a Top 5 Friend?

List the people you knew or know from high school who would consider YOU within their top friends. Are you still close with them? If not, would you consider becoming reacquainted with them?

WHO WOULD CONSIDER YOU A TOP 5 FRIEND?	ARE YOU STILL FRIENDS WITH THEM? (Y/N)	IF NOT, WOULD YOU LIKE TO BE? (Y/N)
1.		
2.		
3.		
4.		
5.		

Friendship in College

For many, the opportunity to go to college is a chance to be completely free of parental monitoring and experience a first taste of adulthood, all while operating in the semi-protected, semi-secure structure of school. You aren't even close to being in the real world yet, but are still able to practice your hand at adulting. Entering college offers many people a fresh start. Perhaps you went to a small school or a boarding school, or just never really found your "people" in high school. College presents an opportunity to completely reinvent yourself. By the time you enter college, you might have had an opportunity to get to know yourself a bit more; for instance, what you like in friends and what you don't like.

Colleges offer more access than high school to different types of people, opportunities, and perspectives. In your classes, you might be surrounded by international students, older students, and younger students. College is just not as restrictive. While your high school friends know who you are on one intimate level (for example, they probably saw your parents discipline you at one point or another), your college friends know you on a whole different level. Those of us who had the privilege of living away from our homes during college lived with strangers—quite honestly a terrifying concept. You sleep in the same room as a stranger, eat with strangers, study with strangers, and party with strangers. In college you're beholden to no one. College students all learn how to become independent and responsible at the same time. Even if you are fortunate enough to know someone from your high school in college,

HERE TO MAKE FRIENDS

you probably don't have the opportunity to see them very often. Nonetheless, college offers a unique bonding opportunity that neither high school nor adulthood (minus the possibility of graduate school) offers. As the months pass, those strangers that you room with, eat with, and study with might end up becoming close friends.

Quick Tip:
Making Friends in College

Why is making friends in college easy for some and not others? We all bring a different combination of numbers to the friendship equation. While the typical equation of A+B=C could work for many, there are never any guarantees that you will end up at "C." That said, sometimes you need to carve out your own road map. Perhaps you are a freshman in college and are having a hard time finding other like-minded people? Instead of searching high and low to find them, consider bringing them to you. Organize a meet-up or a meet-and-greet around a theme you are interested in. College campuses often have student activity committees that create and fund student interest groups. You never know who else might be interested! Also, don't forget life beyond the college walls. Consider exploring other avenues in the local community to connect with other people, such as the local café, bar, or yoga studio.

While the equation for making friends is not altogether different than it is at any other developmental stage—you still need proximity, similarity, and fun—a key difference is that you don't necessarily have the support you once had at home. Your family is no longer available around the clock for you. You must forge different communities and rely on new friends, because it's likely that your besties from high school have moved on too. Additionally, because of reduced reliance on your old support systems, college is a time where people display more prosocial or helping behaviors—a key component of adult friendships. While these behaviors likely existed during your earlier friendships, they are more frequent and supportive in college. Research indicates that there is a strong correlation between such helping behaviors during college and relationship trust.[14] Remember those days when you were cramming for finals and your friend shared their study guide with you? Or when your roommate bunked with a friend because you needed to have the room to yourself for the night? What about when you were a shoulder to cry on for a friend who'd just broken up with their significant other? In thinking about my college years, I can't help but reflect on how many friends' parents I met or how many holiday celebrations I was invited to (even though I didn't celebrate that occasion) because I eventually became a member of the family.

14   Yuan Guo, "The Influence of Social Support on the Prosocial Behavior of College Students: The Mediating Effect Based on Interpersonal Trust," *English Language Teaching* 10, no. 12 (2017): 158, doi:10.5539/elt.v10n12p158.

Another unique factor that aids in the development of long-term friendships in college is the presence of sororities and fraternities. Joining sororities and fraternities in college allows undergraduates to form connections and get involved in social life on campus. Those who decide to rush a sorority or fraternity gain a bonding experience as they go through the recruitment experience. Even if you don't end up pledging to Greek life, you still get the opportunity to meet new people. An underlying organizational premise of Greek life is that you have a de facto family—brothers and sisters of sorts that are able to help you adapt to college life quicker. It's often the case that folks who pledged together during their freshman or sophomore years remain connected well into adulthood.

Greek life is just one example of how college students can make friends. College offers opportunities for everyone to find people like them (at least in one way or another). Unlike high school, college provides a variety of opportunities to socialize and better develop your multiple identities. I would even argue that college life is the ideal place for meeting new people and getting a better sense of who you are and who you want to be in the "real" world. Think of all the clubs, sports teams, and arts opportunities presented to you at college. You could become an intramural volleyball player or a member of the LGBTQ+ alliance, along with several other things—all at the same time! Through those groups college students meet people who are interested in those specific elements of their identity.

Quick Tip:
Tackling New Social Situations for the Socially Anxious

"We all have the same feelings—we just feel them differently and not all at the same time." This is one of my favorite go-to thoughts when I'm feeling insecure or anxious about a new experience. It's true that we have all been in the same shoes at one point or another. Keep this in mind while approaching a new social situation. Also, if you approach a new social situation with a friend you trust, ask them for moral support. If you're alone, practice your social skills by attending gatherings where you know people, and give yourself a time limit. By establishing a time limit, you are giving yourself a boundary and a possible escape plan, which can take the pressure off. So, curious about attending that party where you know no one? Do it, and know that you have an out. If you end up having a good time—good for you!

HERE TO MAKE FRIENDS

Closest College Friends

Some of your closest friends are likely those that you met in college. Below, list the top 5 friends you had in college and compare them to a list of the five people you keep in touch with the most. Are they the same people? Could you imagine contacting those people with whom you don't have a lot of contact?

TOP 5 FRIENDS IN COLLEGE	TOP 5 PEOPLE YOU ARE IN CONTACT WITH FROM COLLEGE	ARE THEY THE SAME?
1.		
2.		
3.		
4.		
5.		

Whom would you would be interested in reconnecting with?

1. _____

2. _____

3. _____

4. _____

5. _____

What are the potential obstacles to reconnecting?

_____

_____

_____

_____

_____

Brainstorm possible ways to overcome these obstacles.

_____

_____

_____

_____

_____

Now that you've had some time to reflect and take a personal inventory of your friend-finding successes and failures, you're probably more aware of how you have made

HERE TO MAKE FRIENDS

friends historically, as well as the role that systems such as schools, families, and communities played in your efforts. If you're an adult who is currently struggling with finding and keeping friends, it's important to have compassion for yourself and realize that it was easier to make friends as a child, thanks in large part to those structured institutions. While there are some outliers—such as children who are homeschooled—even their parents will often work to connect them to a larger community. Most of us have friends that we meet early in life through childhood encounters and playdates organized by our parents. As we developed a sense of who and what we liked, we started to be more selective in choosing our friends. Toward the end of high school and in college, we had a clearer picture of who we were and where we were going. As a result, we started to select friends with similar values to ours and, if we've been lucky, those people have stayed in our lives.

Friendship Now

Friendship in Young Adulthood

If you're reading this book, it is likely that you're an adult struggling to make friends or keep up with the ones you already have. As we learned earlier, the road map for making friends is provided for us in the school-age years, but there doesn't appear to be a map for making friends when you have graduated from these institutions. Unlike past generations, when people were readily accepted into the workforce and had another opportunity to make friends, those coming out of school nowadays often have a different experience.

Quick Tip: Game Day

Practice makes perfect, right? This cliché is TRUE. If you struggle with meeting new people, try striking up a conversation with acquaintances (those people in your life you may know, but don't really *know*). For instance, try to make casual conversation with the barista at your go-to coffee shop, your workout instructor, or even that random person you always see in the elevator. You see these people often enough that they will likely be happy to have a little chat with you now and then. Essentially, these opportunities are low-hanging fruit and can make you feel confident in your abilities to engage with almost anyone. And you never know when other social opportunities might come about. By practicing these techniques on a smaller scale, you're more likely to have success when it counts!

Consider the millennials and Gen Zers whose lives are interconnected with social media, and the impact that this has had on making and sustaining friendships after college. At first glance, it might appear that these individuals are fortunate. Unlike past generations, they can cast a wider net and explore potential friendships from behind a screen. Maybe you've casually met up with someone you kind-of sort-of know from Instagram or Twitter. Maybe you've been introduced to someone via email and afterward set up a coffee date with that person to get to know them better. However, these examples aren't the most common. Thanks to social media, it's easy to stay behind the screen and never take that step of meeting in person. Consider your childhood pen pal. Did you ever meet them in person? Probably not. What happened after the first few letters were sent back and forth? Did it fizzle out? If you're anything like me, it probably did.

Without the constructs of school or work to socialize, we're left to our phones and computers—for better or worse. I recall my own graduation from college. The day after graduation, after the hoopla died, and the parents were gone, and my friends and classmates had packed up and left, it finally dawned on me that, for the first time in my life, I was about to embark on this journey that didn't entail a school or a built-in community. While the prospect was exciting in some regards, it was terrifying in others. Many of my friends had moved out of my college town to embark on their own journeys where they would not know anyone and would need to start fresh. Instead, I had decided to stay in my college town after graduation to start a job, and found that it was different. Some of my local friends were still in college and, while those who moved away were at my fingertips via social media, it just wasn't the same. There I was, 22 years old, starting my first day of work with a group of new folks who were, from my perspective, much older than me. I felt alone, lost, and excited all at once. My experience is a common one. The feelings of instability and of being a little lost after four transformative years of your life is natural. As a therapist, I often receive calls from individuals who have just graduated college, moved to a new city, and are without a formal institution to help them with socializing. Without an institution or anchor to make friends, friendship-finding and -keeping becomes difficult. And for those individuals who struggle with introversion or social anxiety, it can sometimes feel nearly impossible.

Friendship for a Working Adult

Finding friends and making them in young adulthood is different from doing so in other stages of life in that work (where you aren't surrounded by peers of the same age) becomes a substitute for school. While there are some exceptions, many of us moving from college into the work-force find ourselves among colleagues who are older than us. This isn't a bad thing exactly. As many of us learn, we often find like-minded people with similar interests in the workplace. For many who do work in a more traditional workplace environment, this is the best and easiest place to start meeting new people as:

1. You already spend a significant amount of your time at work anyway; and,

2. Everyone likes to swap office gossip and kvetch with their colleagues about workplace practices.

Additionally, since many employers value a positive workplace environment, they often encourage community-building with events such as regular happy hours, team-building activities, and celebrations (e.g., work lunches, office birthday parties). All of these provide opportunities to get to know your colleagues on a more intimate basis, allowing for the possibility of organic friendships. As tech companies and startups continue to rise, we are seeing community-centric offices become more and more popular. Think, foosball tables, beer on tap, and common spaces where people can gather and meet.

The financial access and responsibility of young adulthood also changes the friend-finding process. In college you might not have had a job, and therefore had to rely on your parents for an allowance, if you were lucky. However, as a young adult, you have your own income, which opens many new opportunities. For many, this period of life is marked by dating and meeting up with coworkers and friends at bars and coffee shops. Even though you may have a steady income, college debt and the high cost of living might force you to share an apartment with other young professionals to lessen the burden of monthly rent. For many, this is a great way to meet new people. If you have the good fortune to have decent roommates, they can be a source of support and companionship. Plus, even if you don't have the ideal roommate situation, you never know who you might meet through them.

Of course, we also need to consider those young adults who head back home after college. It's not that uncommon to return to your hometown and live with your parents while you seek employment. If you are in this situation, don't worry, there are still opportunities to meet new people. For some, living at home may mean maintaining a sense of community and strengthening connections with high school acquaintances. For others, it allows the opportunity to pay off student loans or to save up for other experiences.

Today, many more young adults than in previous generations are focused on having lived experiences like traveling, going to concerts, etc. The focus on having these experiences not only aids in your self-development but also your social network. This is one of the benefits of social media: You can stay connected to those you may meet hiking across Europe or at a music festival.

Quick Tip:
Living with Your Parents

If graduating college and finding a job weren't hard enough, life becomes harder if you have to move back in with your parents. Shifting from a semi-autonomous person in college to an actual autonomous adult living with your parents can be a difficult transition, especially if you are trying to meet new people. Some friend-finding tips if you are living with your parents include:

- Set clear boundaries and expectations with your parents so that you don't feel guilty seeking out new opportunities for yourself.

- Use social media to reconnect with people, even those you only knew as acquaintances in high school.

- Join a gym where there may be other people, young and old, like yourself.

- If your parents have a dinner party or BBQ, go to it, even if it's just for a little. Perhaps they will invite people their age who have adult children your age.

Dating

Dating is another way to meet new prospective friends. Whether you are meeting new people through your current bae (your love interest) or your friend's love interest, dating has always been a great way to connect to people that you maybe wouldn't meet in any other situation. I can't help but recall numerous stories of romantic relationships between two lovers that didn't work, but they either became good friends or met their close friends through their partner.

Young adults, unlike their older counterparts, are more apt to take risks when it comes to meeting new people, and seem to be more open to making themselves vulnerable—a key component in the friend-making department. While this may seem like a stretch to some, there's neuroscience to prove it! The prefrontal cortex is the brain's judgment center, and doesn't fully develop until the age of 25 years old. As a result, inhibitions like fear of rejection or embarrassment tend to be less prominent in younger people. As we age, however, the prefrontal cortex develops more fully and we may be less likely to take risks, such as going up to a stranger and introducing ourselves, for fear of looking foolish or being judged. Hence, the ease of making friends as a child with the words "Hey, wanna be my friend?" makes sense.

This is often the case with my clients. When I suggest seeking out a meet-up or a new group opportunity, my younger clients are more likely to follow up on the recommendation. Fear of judgment and the unknown are far greater concerns when I propose the exact same recommendations to those who are older.

That said, younger adults are more likely to leverage social media and put it to use. For instance, they will follow and DM that person they met on vacation or at a concert. For some Gen Zers, the assumption is that if you have connected on Instagram, you *are* friends. There's no, "I know we haven't met in person yet, but I think we'd be fine friends." That hesitant wavering simply doesn't happen. Nonetheless, while there is no clear guarantee that this strategy works out for every person, some young adults today grew up making fast friendships in chat rooms or playing video games with strangers. It is not beyond the realm of possibility for an online relationship to be taken to the next level and for a genuine friendship to develop. The truth is that, in today's friend-finding market there are more opportunities than ever for making friends.

Back to School

Over time, some young adults might find that they need to branch out and make more money, which could mean returning to the best place to make friends...yep, that's right, school. Entering grad school can provide a welcome break from the efforts that go into friend-finding when out in the work world. You're back in a place where you have proximity to like-minded people with similar interests. Graduate school provides a more mature environment where your peers are likely to be your future colleagues. Enduring rigorous academics with a cohort of people not only enables plenty of opportunities to be vulnerable—consider those long all-nighters—but also for others to get to know you on a more intimate level. You can learn a lot about another person while cramming for the Bar exam, working in a lab, or completing a dissertation!

Rate Your Efforts

It is important to recognize that for some, engaging in the more traditional ways to make friends that I've discussed thus far is hard. In this exercise, reflect on what efforts you've made as a young adult to meet new people. List all your efforts, then rate their ease or difficulty on a scale of 1 to 10, with 1 being very, very easy and 10 being most difficult. Then, determine if your efforts were a success! See the example below:

EFFORTS MADE TOWARD MEETING NEW PEOPLE	DIFFICULTY RATING (1 TO 10)	EFFORTS SUCCESSFUL? (Y/N)
Went to a local pub by myself	8.5, difficult	Yes, met 2 people
Talked to staff at yoga studio	3, rather easy	Yes, talked to 3 people
Went to a gallery opening by myself	7, difficult	Yes, talked to 5 people

Now you try....

EFFORTS MADE TOWARD MEETING NEW PEOPLE	DIFFICULTY RATING (1 TO 10)	EFFORTS SUCCESSFUL? (Y/N)

Take note of what actions were easy and which were hard. This will become useful in a future section that discusses your approach and its effectiveness in making friends. If you've found one or two ways that are particularly easy and successful for you, these may be useful strategies for you—good job!

Quick Tip:
"Too Busy" to Make Friends

Life gets in the way of many things—especially important things like building and maintaining relationships. However, relationships are crucial to even the busiest person's well-being. Here are some easy ways to integrate friend-finding, relationship-building, and sustaining friendship into a busy schedule.

- Say yes to at least one invitation out quarterly. If you say no one too many times, you will no longer get the invite.

- Demonstrate reciprocity by inviting others to an event you host at least once a year.

- If you vacation, make it a group vacation. Nothing is better than bringing friends and family together to bond and create a lifetime of memories.

Middle Adulthood

While making and maintaining friends in young adulthood can be challenging, research has found that the number of friendships starts to decrease as we age—which is not surprising. The surprising fact, however, is that the number of friendships starts to decline as early as age 25.[15] On paper this seems almost too early—college graduation seemed like it was yesterday and, at 25 years old, you likely have just started to acclimate to a new job and new friends. While there are likely a variety of factors influencing this decline, the most obvious is that at 25 many people start to look for that one, very special friend—their significant other.

The research asserts that, starting at around age 30, men and women experience the rate of disconnection from friends differently. This change likely stems from the fact that individuals partner off and procreate, therefore limiting the amount of time that parents, in particular women, can connect and engage with their friends. Interestingly, while the number of friends diminishes for both males and females up until age 30, something changes at around age 45 for women—they appear to develop more connections. Between ages 45 and 55, the number of friends for both males and females appears to plateau at a steady rate.[16]

Despite the limitations of this study—close connections/ friendships were measured by phone calls and not in-person contact or communication via social media—it does give us a sense of what happens for many in midlife.

---

15   Kunal Bhattacharya et al., "Sex Differences in Social Focus across the Life Cycle in Humans," *Royal Society Open Science* 3, no. 4 (2016) , doi:10.1098/rsos.160097.

16   Bhattacharya et al., "Sex Differences in Social Function across the Life Cycle in Humans."

Perhaps at this point in your life you have found the "one" or the "one for right now." As is typical in the early stages of love, you are completely enamored and infatuated. You're probably not thinking about your weekly lunch date with your besties and maybe you skip that party or that golf game to hang out with your partner.

Or perhaps your friends are now partnered and, rather than playing the third wheel, you focus completely on your career. Suddenly you find yourself in the cruel world of full-on adulting. Life and your friendships are just different from how they were when you graduated high school and college. You may be navigating and negotiating your love life, your work life, and mounting financial obligations (hello student loans). Oy! Nonetheless, there just never seems like enough time to connect.

Middle-adulthood is complicated and, after the daily tasks of living are completed (e.g., paying rent, mortgage, bills, taking care of children, etc.), there's not a lot of energy left to do much else. As a result, this is, for many people, the most challenging time to maintain friendships. Instead, many turn to what we earlier termed kinship-friendship. Instead of relying on outside friends, they look toward relatives for support and companionship. Although having familial support is a strength and a protective factor for some, others lack it. Those who do not have time to maintain their previous friends and do not have the support of family can become isolated, with no one else but their significant other to look toward. This can and often does happen without many even noticing that their social network has diminished.

Research from the *British Medical Journal* indicates that diminished social networks for both men and women in midlife can have profound implications on mental health.[17] Findings indicated that, compared to those individuals who had 10 or more connections/friends, women with smaller networks of friends at age 45 had significantly lower levels of psychological well-being. Interestingly, the impact of fewer connections appeared to adversely impact women more than it did men. Women who pursued longer-term education appeared to have larger friendship networks than their male counterparts—again, we see the school theme. What mattered more for the well-being of men in this study was the extent of their familial networks.

Finding and keeping friendship at midlife is critical to one's well-being—but do not worry. There are opportunities even at this stage of life to course-correct. The easiest way to connect with new people and find possible friends lies in schools or school-like institutions. Many adults pursue interest classes in wine tasting, cooking, or athletics to enhance their socialization skills and meet like-minded

17 Noriko Cable et al., "Friends Are Equally Important to Men and Women, but Family Matters More for Mens' Well-Being," *Journal of Epidemiology and Community Health* 67, no. 2 (2012): 166–171, doi:10.1136/jech-2012-201113.

people. While participation in these activities doesn't always guarantee meeting your next bestie, it's likely you will find a companion or two with whom you can be active and engaged. New parents often find connecting with old friends difficult to do, let alone meeting new ones. Those who make efforts to socialize with other new parents often find it easy to connect with individuals experiencing similar life-course changes. Some ways new parents do this are by joining parenting groups, play groups, or educational seminars.

Eventually, as children age, it becomes easier for parents to have more opportunities to socialize again, often with the parents of their children's friends. While this may not be every parent's ideal way to meet new people, it is yet another way that new connections are accessible. In communities where the school system serves as an anchor, it's very likely that if you befriend your children's friends' parents, you will be friends with them in years to come. Consider those stories of parents who were invited to a wedding of their adult children's friends. Or a family event where your parents' besties were the parents of someone you knew from school.

Quick Tip:
The Out-of-Practice Person

Whether you are old or young, socializing takes practice. Perhaps when you were younger you found it easier to get up and start a conversation with anyone, but now, between long hours of work and other adult responsibilities, it seems extra exhausting. Even the thought of striking up a conversation with someone is enough to make you want to sleep for days—but there's hope.

Often, people are reluctant to engage in a conversation because they fear that they will have to say something meaningful. People become focused on what they are going to say instead of listening. The key trick here is to remember that most people like talking about themselves, and most people don't have good listeners around them. So, be that good listener.

How Connected Are You?

Given the multiple realities of midlife—career, kids, paying debt, intimate partners, caring for aging parents—there is little time to collect new friends and stay in contact with old friends. Even if you aren't in your midlife yet, the exercise below aims to help you identify just how well you are doing with staying connected to your old friends compared to your newer friends, and provides you with an opportunity to make some changes, if needed.

Write down the names of the last five people with whom you made contact (communication can be via phone, text, IM, DM, Slack).

1. _____

2. _____

3. _____

4. _____

5. _____

Are there patterns in these communications? For instance, were the last five contacts you had with another person the same person? Or, was there diversity in whom you contacted? Maybe the last few contacts include your partner, your parent, or your boss. Think about who else you would want to be on that list—would it be a friend that you haven't seen or heard from in a while? Could you imagine what it would be like to reach out to them right now and tell them that you have been thinking about them? What about that prospective acquaintance you were recently introduced to—could you use this as an opportunity to connect with them?

Friendship in Older Adulthood

No matter your age when reading this book, I think it's important to include a section on friendship in older adulthood. Maybe you're an older adult reading this book at the recommendation of some younger adult, or maybe you're reading this book because you too are struggling with making friends. Regardless of your reasoning, it's important to think about friendship throughout the many different stages of life so that when you arrive at each stage you are well-prepared and informed of the possible friendship challenges that lie ahead. The truth is that, the sooner you start investing and cultivating your friendships, the better off you will be in the long run. So, make a choice to be ahead of the game and work to develop your friendships now, while also planning for your future friendships.

As with any age, friendship in later life, which for the purposes of this book we will consider age 65 and older, is instrumental in one's mental and physical well-being, and it is not that different from friendships at other points in one's life-course. In fact, older adults often have very similar expectations of their friends now as they did during late adolescence.[18] Research has found that older adults still define a close friend as someone who provides emotional and practical support, and someone you can talk to and

18 Williams Rawlins, "Friendships in Later Life," in *LEA's Communication Series. Handbook of Communication and Aging Research* (Mahwah, NJ: Lawrence Erlbaum Associates Publishers, 2004).

enjoy spending time with. One primary difference between friendship in older adulthood as compared to other stages of life is that friendship in the later years tends to focus more on personal well-being.

Quick Tip:
Older Adults

An important factor for anyone's well-being, especially older adults, is continuity. For instance, building in regular opportunities for socialization, whether it's walking your dog, going to a book club, attending religious events, or volunteering, help maintain a sense of community and a feeling of being understood. Volunteering or being helpful to others can foster a sense of positive regard and create other opportunities for friendship. Helping a neighbor out with their children or pets allows multiple opportunities to get to know someone on a more intimate level.

Take the case of Jane, a widow with adult children who lived out of town. Jane would occasionally help babysit her neighbor's children and, over time, became an integral part of their family. Jane gained a friend and so did her neighbor.

Despite the many commonalities, friendships as an older adult do come with some striking differences. First, older adults may have fewer opportunities to find new friends, or they become choosier when it comes to picking new friends. I recall one grandmother's pointed feedback about expanding her social network. She commented that, at her age, it was more important to cherish the friendships she had than invest in new ones. To some extent, she was right. Throughout our lives we are selective in whom we keep in our circles. As you get older and value your time more, it makes sense to simply focus on those existing friendships.

Interestingly, the research indicates that there might be some nuanced differences in friendships between older men and women. According to psychologist Geoffrey Greif, women's relationships are more intimate and require more emotional maintenance, whereas male friendships appear to be "shoulder-to-shoulder" encounters, meaning that emotional needs of men are more easily fulfilled by watching a show or doing something together.[19]

Retirement is a common life-course transition that may impact older adults' ability to sustain and build new friendships. While some of these friendships persist, finding friendship without the anchor of the workplace takes a lot of effort! As a result, many older adults, if they want to meet new people or maintain their work friendships, will have to engage in other activities. This can be challenging

---

19 Geoffrey L. Greif, *Buddy System: Understanding Male Friendships* (New York: Oxford University Press, 2009).

for some who didn't work to cultivate those friendships earlier on. In treatment, clients often speak of how they'd dedicated themselves to work or to their families only to find themselves without much to do and no one to do stuff with once they retire. For some, the thought of putting themselves out there to pursue new activities and meet new people is daunting.

Physical, financial, and health constraints may also create barriers to friendship, as they may cause older adults to move from the communities and homes where they developed their social networks. Loss of independence combined with other losses typical in older adulthood—such as the death of friends or a spouse, or relocation—may also impact older adults' ability to socialize and connect with others. For those with limited connections, the focus often turns to kinship friendship—friendship found within the extended family system. Although social networks dwindle over time, the literature points to one main factor that matters the most—the quality of the existing connections, or the ways in which older adults experience companionship, pleasure, and reciprocity in their friendships.[20]

The truth is that with the advent of social media there appear to be more similarities among older adults and their younger counterparts. While baby boomers may not

20   Karen A. Roberto and Jean P. Scott, "Friendships of Older Men and Women: Exchange Patterns and Satisfaction," *Psychology and Aging* 1, no. 2 (1986): 103–109, doi:10.1037/0882-7974.1.2.103.

be on Instagram at the same rate or frequency as millennials or Gen Zers, they are the fastest-growing demographic on social media. Facebook (and even Instagram) are great ways for older adults to stay connected to friends who have moved away. It can also be a great place to connect to long-lost friends—think of stories about childhood best friends reconnecting over DM.

While social media can be a nice supplement for long-distance friendships, it does not and should not take the place of face-to-face meetings. The risk of using social media as a substitute for real-life, face-to-face interactions can be harmful. Using Facebook or Instagram as your only platform to connect with people is isolating and unhealthy for one's mental health—we have all heard that overuse of social media can contribute to depressive symptoms; for older adults, using only social media platforms to socialize can lead to less physical activity and poor overall health. The impact that social media has on our brain's reward system causes many people to fall into a vicious cycle of clicking and repeating—rechecking Facebook every five minutes. The consequence here is when there are no new likes to your post, you don't get that dopamine (the happy hormone) hit, which can make you feel worse, especially if your only connections are virtual.

Rate Your Current Connections

Now that you understand the research on friendship, connections, and older adulthood, this exercise aims to help you reflect on where and how you are engaging with your current connections. Considering that in-person connections and the quality of those connections are what matter the most, list your five most recent in-person interactions and rate them on scale of 1 to 10, with 1 being terrible and 10 being amazing:

FIVE MOST RECENT IN-PERSON INTERACTIONS	EXPERIENCE RATING
1.	
2.	
3.	
4.	
5.	

What was your best in-person interaction? Ask yourself why it was the best. Is there a way that you could re-create your most positive interaction? What role did you have in that interaction? What was your least favorite in-person interaction? What caused that interaction to not be as favorable as the others? What was your contribution to that interaction, and could you have done anything to change that outcome?

Summary

There's no doubt that, while making friends as a child, teen, and student is hard, it certainly becomes more nuanced and time-consuming as you reach the various stages of adulthood. The complexities of adulthood can leave anyone feeling isolated, vulnerable, and alone. However, you are not alone in this struggle, and if you are patient, maintain hope, and are reflective, you can feel secure that you do not have to be alone or isolated.

The predominant theme in making friends throughout young-adulthood, middle-adulthood, and older adulthood is that success comes from vulnerability. You must learn to be open and vulnerable in order to find new friends and maintain your old ones. When you are comfortable with being vulnerable, this gives you the courage needed to go to a gathering where you know no one, or to contact a long-lost friend and simply say, "Hey, I have been thinking about you."

Historically, vulnerability has been a dirty word, often associated with one's weaknesses. Being vulnerable in a society where cliques and competitiveness are valued seems like an oxymoron; however, it is the key to making friends. You can't reap the benefits from a true friendship if you refuse to give yourself equally to the relationship. Keeping walls up and pretending to be someone you're not allows for a friendship to be built on falsehoods. But when you're vulnerable and truthful, a deeply precious relationship can be formed. As this book continues to unravel the secrets and skills to making and keeping meaningful friendships, I will ask you to be vulnerable. I will show you how to be appropriately vulnerable so as to allow others into your world and invite you into theirs.

CHAPTER 3

YOUR FRIENDSHIP PERSONALITY TYPE

If you've made it to this point in the book, you've likely completed a few of the exercises examining where you are in your friendship journey. Maybe you've realized that you're acing the friendship game and have plenty of quality, meaningful friendships. Perhaps these exercises have been useful in pinpointing the specific gaps in your friendships—maybe you have too many friendships of the good and not enough friends of utility. As a result of such self-examination, you may realize that, even with the number of friendships and connections you have, they still do not soothe that feeling of loneliness you are experiencing.

Alone vs. Lonely

There is a nuanced difference between being alone and feeling lonely, and it is important to differentiate the two. Aloneness is the experience of being by one's self, which can be refreshing, restorative, and therapeutic for some. Aloneness can devolve into feelings of loneliness when being alone becomes intolerable and you want to connect with other people but are struggling.

We all experience moments of both aloneness and loneliness. In fact, you can experience loneliness even when you are not alone. Have you ever had a moment when you were with people you know and like but just couldn't connect to them? In that moment you might feel lonely, and this feeling might be incredibly painful. Unfortunately, this is a very, very common experience that many millions of others also experience. Statistics indicate that, at almost any given time, nearly half of Americans feel lonely, and that these feelings impact more younger people than older people.[21]

Feeling lonely in the age of social media can lead to a more-is-more approach: going on an Instagram following spree or swiping right on every option on Tinder. But more is not always more. Some struggling with loneliness may have 5, 15, or even 50 quality connections and still feel

21   Knowledge Network and Insight Policy Research, "Loneliness among Older Adults," accessed May 10, 2019, https://assets.aarp.org/rgcenter/general/loneliness_2010.pdf.

HERE TO MAKE FRIENDS

lonely. Others will jump at any opportunity for companionship and find themselves spending time with people they don't like, which only exacerbates their feelings of loneliness and unhappiness.

Quick Tip:
You Are Not Alone

Lonesomeness is best described as the feeling you have when you would like to have companionship but can't. Think about when you want to hang out with some friends on a Friday night, but everyone is busy but you. While watching Netflix alone may be a bummer, it is temporary.

Loneliness is different from lonesomeness because it is chronic—it is a feeling that is always there.

Chronic loneliness is quite common. Studies on loneliness reveal that:[22]

- Nearly half of adults in the US report feeling lonely or left out.

- Gen Z, people born between 1997 and 2013, appears to be the loneliest generation.

---

22 Cigna, "New Cigna Study Reveals Loneliness at Epidemic Levels in America," accessed May 11, 2019, https://www.cigna.com/newsroom/news-releases/2018/new-cigna-study-reveals-loneliness-at-epidemic-levels-in-america.

- Millennials, people born between 1981 and 1996, were the second loneliest generation.

- Older generations were found to experience loneliness at lower rates.

Sometimes feelings of loneliness stem from factors other than a lack of friends or quality friendships. For some, there's no clear or obvious reason for feeling lonely. However, a number of factors may contribute to an adult's experience of loneliness that are unrelated to social circle, and are instead connected to early childhood experiences, misattuned parents, or relational trauma. Such specific causes are best illuminated and treated in therapy with properly trained therapists.

Quick Tip:
Remembering to Be Mindful

Everyday life is busy and, if you are like most people, you find yourself running from one place to another. Very few of us make the time to slow down and smell the roses. As a result, we often miss a multitude of opportunities for connection. Perhaps you were too busy texting someone in the elevator when there may have been an opportunity to chitchat with the person next to you. Or maybe when you were running to your car this morning you were in such a rush that you didn't notice your neighbor trying to say hello. Slowing down does matter. One of my mentors once reminded me that the slower you go, the more progress you make.

One way to go slow is to practice mindful walking. The goal of mindful walking is to simply enjoy walking. In this practice, walk aimlessly, taking notice of how your feet pound the pavement, the movement of the trees and wind above you, and the people moving past you. Take time to physically slow down so that you don't miss potential opportunities for connection.

Alone or Lonely?

All of us have times when we feel alone, lonely, or both. However, for most of us, it is hard to discern what we are feeling from what we are experiencing, especially if you are on the more introverted side. This exercise aims to assess if you are at risk of feeling alone and/or lonely.

DO YOU:	YES/NO (If yes, how often?)
Feel alone in a crowd of people?	
Crave human attention?	
Feel that no one can understand you?	

DO YOU:	YES/NO (If yes, how often?)
Always feel left out?	
Feel sad or depressed?	
Feel like you are a part of a group?	

Count the number of times you answered yes to these questions. More "yes" answers with a high frequency of these feelings places you at a greater risk of loneliness. There are many millions of people who are struggling with the same feelings and, if you are one of them, you may want to pay close attention to these signs and seek professional support from a mental health counselor, therapist, or life coach.

Combating Loneliness

By now you have likely determined when you are alone and when you don't want to be. The harder part of this equation is addressing your loneliness. We know that, for some, feelings of loneliness go deeper than one's social network and that addressing the deeper roots of loneliness stemming from trauma and early childhood may take some time and professional help.

Quick Tip:
Self-Compassion

Dr. Kristen Neff, an expert and researcher in the field of self-compassion, suggests that one way to develop more compassion for yourself is to treat yourself as you would a friend.[23] This self-compassion exercise expounded on from Dr. Neff's "Self-Compassion Exercise 1: How Would You Treat a Friend?" is beneficial for several reasons, as it can help you determine the type of friend you are to yourself and the type of friend you would be to others. Consider how you treat or would treat friends when they are down or are feeling unwell. A good friend would likely treat them with warmth, kindness, empathy, and understanding. Consider what you might say. How would you demonstrate care? What would you do to help? How would you express your support? Would your tone be sympathetic? Airy? Condescending? Somber? Playful?

If you were to write your answers down, do you think they would be similar to how you might respond to a friend in the same situation? If you are like most of us, you are probably not as kind to yourself as you would be to a friend. Take note of this advice: If you can't have compassion for yourself no one else will!

---

23 Kristin Neff, "Self-Compassion Exercise 1: How Would You Treat a Friend?" accessed July 11, 2019, https://self-compassion.org/exercise-1-treat-friend.

You are probably wondering how you might be able to cope with the feelings of loneliness on your own as you journey to find quality, meaningful friendships. See the suggestions below on ways that you can combat or minimize feelings of loneliness:

1. Practice self-compassion. The first step to combating loneliness is to look inward and remind yourself that even if you're suffering, you're not alone. Remind yourself of the statistics. Try not to beat yourself up and enter a negative narrative about the cause of your feelings. Try to identify *what is working*. Even if you feel like there's nothing, that's just not true. *There is always something.*

You don't have to identify something huge that's working, just one or two small things. Maybe you woke up on time before the alarm clock this morning. Perhaps your commute to work wasn't an absolute nightmare, or your boss is out and you can leave work a little bit early. Maybe you saw a cute dog on your way home, and it made you smile. Noticing small things that make you happy helps you to be kinder to yourself. For instance, when I am struggling—maybe my Friday night dinner plan ditched me for someone else, or I had an argument with my colleague—I try to reflect on the positive things, even if it is the *smallest* positive thing, that happened before the negative experience. Maybe the sun is out or maybe I had my favorite snack or got to have a positive interaction with someone. I take a

HERE TO MAKE FRIENDS

mental note of these small positive things and tally them. I then remember how these positive experiences made me feel, which is helpful in mitigating some of those negative feelings brought on by being ditched or arguing with someone.

2. Be present. This is the single hardest thing to do for anyone, especially if you aren't feeling great. Most people want to do everything EXCEPT stay present when they are feeling down. Improving your ability to stay in the present moment will enable you to be more attuned to others and the world around you. Meditation and daily practices in mindfulness can help achieve this goal. You may want to try a daily breathing exercise or walking mindfully. Sometimes mantras—or sayings—will help you stay in the moment as well. Some of my favorite mantras are "Nothing is permanent," "Neither the good nor the bad," "I am here in the now," and "No two moments are the same."

3. Be human at least once a day. A very wise person who was juggling school, work, and a family once told me that the key to reducing their risk of social isolation from others was to "do something human once a day." By doing something "human," they meant to get out of their space. It can be easy to stay in your own personal bubble, but this tends to increase feelings of loneliness. Whether it is going to the supermarket or filling up your tank at the gas station, make sure you have at least one outing per day where you can connect with someone in person in another physical space.

4. Say yes to everything (or at least as much as you can). There's an old saying that if you never say yes to an invite, you will stop getting the invitation. Unfortunately, this is true; if you are the person who always opts out you may never get back that opportunity. While this can be hard to do if you are feeling lonely or are suffering from an emotional low where your gut instinct may be to crawl into bed and binge Netflix, fight the bad feeling! Consider the case of Ashley, a friend of mine who wasn't quite ready to hit the town again after spending several months recuperating from major surgery at her parents' home. The easier road for her would have been to take her time and pass up invites, but she started to feel lonely and was determined not to let this feeling or her surgery set her further back. Though she was tired and out of practice, she started accepting invitations to brunch, a tennis match, going to see a band play, etc. All of this was a challenge for Ashley, who was also on the introverted side, but in the end, she ended up meeting a boyfriend, three friends, and expanding her social network. It is fair to say that Ashley's new mantra "Just say yes" worked! It is also fair to say that as a result of this experience Ashley was able to kill a few birds with one stone—also she is far less introverted now than she had been!

5. Book yourself. A schedule helps you feel organized and can even give you a sense of purpose. Most of our days are consumed with work schedules, but free time is equally important. Booking your free time doesn't have to be cumbersome. It will allow you to build in opportunities for mindfulness, being human every day, and socializing. Instead of idly wondering how you are going to plan next Saturday and risk spending too much time online or watching TV, consider scheduling time to go to a museum or a movie. Schedule time to make your favorite dinner or precook the week's lunches. I guarantee that you will feel more productive, more purposeful, and, hopefully, more efficacious.

6. Limit your screen time. We all fall victim to internet deep dives on our devices, and most of us spend too much time on the screen. Data from the market-research group Nielsen indicates that American adults spend more than 11 media consoles.[24] This fact alone provides answers as to why so many people are struggling with in-person connections. If you are like the many other Americans struggling with a screen addiction, your sense of loneliness may be reduced if you reduce time spent on screens. The less you

---

24   Quentin Fottrell, "People Spend Most of Their Waking Hours Staring at Screens," MarketWatch, August 04, 2018, https://www.marketwatch.com/story/people-are-spending-most-of-their-waking-hours-staring-at-screens-2018-08-01.

are on your screen, the more engaged you will be with others and the world around you.

7. Be intentional with your screen time. In an ideal world, you would both reduce your screen time and use it more mindfully. Using screen time mindfully means using it with intentionality. As mentioned above, we have all been caught in that vicious cycle of aimlessly surfing the internet. Like the walking mindfully exercise, using screen time with intention calls for a purpose to the screen usage. Consider these questions before picking up your device again today: What am I hoping to achieve from my next encounter with the internet? Can I use this time to reconnect with someone? How much of my time will be spent scrolling, liking, and swiping? Is there something else I should or could be doing? Would I feel better doing those things or surfing the internet?

8. Get a pet or play with someone else's. While this may not be an option for everyone, pet ownership improves mood and feelings of loneliness. Research indicates that people who live alone and have a pet have better overall outcomes.[25] Though pets cannot fully replace the social support you get from human interaction, research indicates that pet ownership is helpful and that pets can oftentimes provide emotional support. In fact, for many

25   Jessica Saunders et al., "Exploring the Differences between Pet and Non-pet Owners: Implications for Human-animal Interaction Research and Policy," *Plos One* 12, no. 6 (2017):, doi:10.1371/journal.pone.0179494.

pet owners, having a pet promotes social interaction and ways to reduce loneliness. Having a pet means going to the pet store, the vet, and, if you are a dog owner, walking the dog. In my own experience as a dog owner, the simple act of taking my dog out for a walk promotes plenty of unsolicited, easy conversations. Consider the dog the icebreaker. Even if you are not able to own your own dog, you can still get these benefits by watching a neighbor's pet, visiting a cat café, or volunteering at an animal shelter.

9. Tell someone. Consider talking to someone close to you about your feelings. This practice in being vulnerable with another person may help you build a stronger connection with them. Additionally, if you share your feelings with someone that cares about you, they might be able to offer you some social and emotional support. Years ago, I was working with Jon, a young man who had moved to New York City after college and had very demanding work hours. In fact, most of his time was spent at work, and he had very little free time. Jon wasn't the type of person who needed a lot of socialization; in fact, at times he liked being alone, but over time too much aloneness turned into loneliness. Jon mustered up the courage to tell a few close friends from college how he was struggling and, much to his surprise, they showed up for him. Jon's friends made more of an effort to text him, visit him, and integrate him within their existing NYC networks. Not only did talking about his feelings make Jon feel better in the end, but his courage to be vulnerable allowed him to create deeper, more meaningful friendships.

10. Start dreaming. For some this may seem like an unreasonable request, especially if you are feeling low, but envisioning how you want your life to be helps. In fact, daydreaming and fantasizing have been found to lift people's moods. Dreaming can be a very cathartic exercise and can provide temporary solace from a challenging situation. When you dream or visualize your life being different, your brain does mini visualization exercises throughout the day, causing you to make micro-changes toward that goal. Can you imagine how you might feel if you were to say yes to that invite or attend a work happy hour? If you could fantasize about who you want in your world, would you be more inclined to call them or respond to their text the next time they reached out?

11. Get rid of those NUTs. Before getting into what the heck NUTs are, you must first understand the feedback loop that exists between thoughts, feelings, and behaviors. Rooted in the origins of cognitive behavioral therapy is the idea that if you can intervene at any one of these three levels—the thought level, the feeling level, or the behavioral level—you can change the way you think, feel, and behave. If you're suffering from loneliness, it's possible that you may be experiencing: Negative Unconscious Thoughts, or

NUTs, a term coined by prominent psychologist and happiness expert Dr. Elisha Goldstein.[26]

NUTs

NUTs live with us beneath our awareness and include deep-rooted beliefs. Examples of NUTs as they relate to feelings of loneliness are: "I am unworthy of friends," "Who would ever be my friend?" or "I will always feel alone." Such negative unconscious thoughts elicit negative feelings, such as depression, and further influence one's isolating behaviors. So how would one change this negative feedback loop? First, one would start with reversing or reframing those initial negative thoughts into positive ones. Take, for instance, the statement: "Who would want to be my friend?" That negative thought can be reframed as, "A lot of people would like to be my friend." Consider the impact of thinking, "A lot of people would want to be my friend" could have on your feelings and behaviors. The hope is that such a positive automatic thought would then elicit a positive feeling and a positive behavior.

---

26 Elisha Goldstein, Uncovering Happiness: *Overcoming Depression with Mindfulness and Self-Compassion* (New York: Atria Books, 2015).

THE COGNITIVE FEEDBACK LOOP

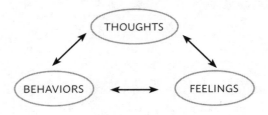

Name Your NUTs

By naming your NUTs, you not only bring awareness to them, but you are also taking the first step to getting rid of them. This is an important skill as, without an understanding of our negative unconscious thoughts, we will not be able to counter and reframe them. With practice, reframing your thoughts will help you move out of your comfort zone and into new territories where you can make friends. In the section below, name those negative thoughts that are getting in the way of your making connections. Then, in the next column, identify a reframe or a reverse to your negative thoughts.

NAME YOUR NEGATIVE THOUGHTS	REVERSE THOSE NEGATIVE THOUGHTS

NAME YOUR NEGATIVE THOUGHTS	REVERSE THOSE NEGATIVE THOUGHTS

If reversing those negative thoughts was hard for you, don't fret, because it is hard for everyone, especially because in our culture we tend to focus more on the negative than the positive. Changing your mindset to focus on the things that are working can be a difficult, but it's a necessary shift to improve your current situation. If you identify with this predicament, I recommend taking the next step and creating your own vision board.

Fans of the Rhonda Byrne's *The Secret* know that the idea behind a vision board is that the more you think about your hopes and dreams, the more positive energy you will put out into the universe, allowing for the manifestation of those hopes and dreams. Vision boards help you visualize your desires and spark motivation to achieve those goals.

Vision boards have been known to work for many. If you are experiencing periods of loneliness, conceptualizing a vision for your life may offer some comfort. You don't need much to create your own vision board. The key to a strong vision board is to include visual representations of how you want to feel. For instance, if you want to feel less lonely, your vision board may display images of people with whom you want to have stronger connections. If you want to be more confident in the workplace, your vision board may include a motivational saying.

While vision boards are useful in helping your brain build awareness and passively take actions toward your goals, action boards help you accomplish your goals faster. Unlike a vision board, action boards require that you put dates on your vision and ideas on how to achieve it. Like a to-do list, an action board provides a road map for how and when to achieve your goals.

Quick Tip:
Kick Those NUTs Out of Your Head!

Practice makes perfect when it comes to kicking those negative unconscious thoughts out of your head. You must consistently practice kicking them out and replacing them with more positive thoughts. As a society, we are conditioned to think in the negative—to first consider what isn't working instead of what is working. This is why we don't always realize when we're in a negative space and need to snap out of it. If this is you, one recommendation is to wear an elastic hair tie or wrist band. When you start to notice that you are going into a negative space, snap the band! By snapping the band, you are bringing yourself back into the present, giving yourself a chance to reframe that negative thought into a positive one.

Another method is to ban negative thoughts from your head. You might think that this is impossible. Consider telling a negative thought to "scram" or "get out of here" the next time it tries to seep in. Someone once told me that the way they were able to kick negative thoughts out was to tell themselves the old adage, "If you don't have anything nice to say, don't say it at all," which prevented her from entertaining any negative thoughts about herself!

How We Make, Maintain, and Break Friendships

New research indicates that, while today's adults are more socially connected than ever before, they also report more profound feelings of loneliness than other generations. A new study conducted by OnePoll in conjunction with Evite determined that the average American hasn't made a new friend in five years, and 45 percent of the adults surveyed reported that it was a challenge to make new friends.[27] Two of the top reasons cited for struggling to make friends is the tendency to be shy or introverted, or experiencing social anxiety in new and uncommon situations. If you experience social anxiety or introversion, take comfort in the fact that you are not alone with this struggle! In the following section, we will try to tease apart some of the internal reasons why it may be hard for you to make friends.

A frequent complaint I hear about the struggle to make friends is that shyness or introversion blocks the energy to meet new people. Sometimes people also feel that the expenditure of that energy just isn't worth it, especially if they haven't been having a lot of success finding positive interactions. Yet, on top of those feelings of pointlessness and dejection, these same people express how desperate they are for connection and comfort with others. The reality is that we are all human, and that means we are interdependent—whether we like it or not. We all need and want friends.

You might be asking yourself: What is keeping me in this dejected mindset? One of the major factors could be the people who raised you. That's right, our ability to make

_____

27 Gervis Zoya, "Why the Average American Hasn't Made a New Friend in 5 Years," *New York Post*, May 10, 2019, https://nypost.com/2019/05/09/why-the-average-american-hasnt-made-a-new-friend-in-5-years.

friends and connect with others, much like our ability to connect and sustain romantic relationships, is influenced by our relationships with our parents. New research suggests that one's attachment style—believed to be instrumental in romantic and familial relationships—is also crucial in understanding how people connect, maintain, and dismantle friendships. In fact, by identifying a person's attachment style, you can predict not only their in-person connections but their online connections.[28]

Attachment Theory and Its Impact on Friendships

Attachment theory and the concept of attachment styles are based on the research of English psychiatrist John Bowlby, who in the 1950s studied broken familial bonds following World War I. He noticed that the war had caused many young British children to have disrupted or broken bonds with their parents. He also examined the well-being of children who had been hospitalized for surgery and were away from their parents for prolonged periods of time.[29] Based on his observations, Bowlby developed a theory that humans have an innate desire to make emotional

---

28 Omri Gillath, Gery Karantzas, and Juwon Lee, "Attachment and Social Networks," *Current Opinion in Psychology*, February 2019. doi: 10.1016/j.copsyc.2018.02.010.

29 David Hruschka, *Friendship: Development, Ecology, and Evolution of a Relationship* (Berkeley, CA: University of California Press, 2010), 377.

attachments and that having strong emotional connections increased infants' and children's survival rates. These positive early childhood attachments would then provide a foundation for developing loving relationships later in life.

Bowlby's research was expounded on in the 1960s when American psychologist Mary Ainsworth conducted the "strange situation" experiment.[30] If you have ever taken an intro psychology course, you are probably familiar with Ainsworth's research. In the strange situation experiment, the researcher takes a mother and her child into a room with toys. The mother leaves, and then the researcher observes the child's behavior. The researcher then records the child's behavior when the parent returns and classifies the child into one of three categories: securely attached, anxious, and avoidant. About two-thirds of the children were classified as *securely attached*, or minorly distressed in their mother's absence but soothed when she returned. One in ten children were observed to be *avoidant*, meaning that they did not become distressed when their mother left, and they avoided her upon return. The researchers found that approximately one-quarter of the children were *anxious*, meaning that they became highly distressed when their mother left, and when their mother returned, they

---

30 Mary D. Salter Ainsworth, Mary Blehar, Everett Waters, and Sally N. Wall. *Patterns of Attachment: A Psychological Study of the Strange Situation*. (New York: Routledge, Taylor & Francis Group, 2015).

HERE TO MAKE FRIENDS

appeared to be ambivalent, crying and reaching for her but then wanting to be let go.

Children in each of these three categories navigate the world differently. Securely attached children know that they have a home base and that they will receive consistent love from their parents. As a result, securely attached children can explore the world freely and know that they can count on their parents for comfort and protection in times of stress. Insecurely attached children—those who either have an avoidant or anxious attachment—struggle with freely exploring their environments. The anxiously attached child is constantly in need of their parent's connection whereas the avoidantly attached child also does not explore and does not demonstrate a need for their parent.

These three categories of attachment don't simply disappear after the child grows up. In fact, they were found to inform how those adults connected to their romantic partners and friends. Adults who were securely attached as kids are those who demonstrate little anxiety and avoidant behaviors in their relationships. Avoidant behaviors in relationships may look like disinterest, lack of engagement, or an overreliance on themselves and not others in relationships. Securely attached adults find it easy to become emotionally close to and depend on others. Being single or alone doesn't worry them, and when they're in a relationship, they don't worry about being rejected. Adults in the anxious attachment category want to be close to their partners, but the fear of being rejected or abandoned is so great that they find it difficult to get closer. Anxiously attached adults are often preoccupied with the worry that they will not be valued as much as they value others. Individuals who have avoidant attachments often feel uncomfortable having emotionally close and intimate relationships for fear that, if they trust or depend on others, they will be hurt. Despite their fear of becoming too close to others, those with avoidant attachments really want intimacy and closeness in their relationships.

Some research on friendship suggests that our attachment styles also apply to the way we make and maintain friendships.[31] Taylor Sixsmith, author of *Steps to Making Friends*, found that securely attached individuals, those who demonstrated little anxiety and avoidant behaviors in their intimate relationships, were more likely to have better relationships with their friends because they had fewer conflicts and were less likely to get jealous. On the other hand, individuals who are categorized as having an insecure attachment style, those with anxious and avoidant attachments, were found to struggle with maintaining their friendships. People under the anxious category were more likely to have others cut ties with them, while

---

31 Omri Gillath, Gery Karantzas, and Juwon Lee, "Attachment and Social Networks," *Current Opinion in Psychology* (February 2019): 21–25.

avoidant people were more likely to do the disconnecting themselves. Secure individuals were found to have more close, quality friendships.

The average person has three to five people in their inner-most circle. Compare this to securely attached people, who have an average of seven people in their innermost circle. Those who have insecure attachments were found to have, on average, fewer than two people in their inner circle.[32]

There are multiple possible reasons for why those with inse-cure attachments—either anxious or avoidant—may have fewer close connections than those with secure relation-ships. One is that anxiously attached people create conflict within friendships because of their fear of rejection, and these conflicts cause the friendships to end. Those who are avoidantly attached may keep prospective new friends at bay, fearing that they will become too close and will be rejected.

---

32 Angela C. Rowe and Katherine B. Carnelley, "Preliminary Support for the Use of a Hierarchical Mapping Technique to Examine Attachment Networks," *Personal Relationships* 12, no. 4 (2005): 499–519, https://doi.org/10.1111/j.1475-6811 .2005.00128.x.

Your Attachment Style

Complete the exercise below by circling the statements that most accurately describe you. Having more circles in a specific category may be an indicator of your attachment style. For some, attachment styles differ depending on the relationship. For instance, you may be more anxious with your lover and more secure in your friendships. See the list of behaviors below to help identify whether you are more secure or anxious/avoidant. Please note that this list does not include all the behaviors that may be signs of your attachment style.

ANXIOUS ATTACHMENT	AVOIDANT ATTACHMENT	SECURE ATTACHMENT
You worry that your intimate others will stop loving/caring about you.	You feel uncomfortable when others get too close.	You are confident in your relationship; you don't question your friendships or relationships.
You typically worry that others will not feel the same way as you do for them.	You find it hard to support others when they are feeling down.	You typically are there for others and if they don't feel the same way for you as you do for them, you are okay with that.
Being involved in relationships, especially romantic ones, helps you feel calm and complete.	You prefer relying on yourself rather than relying on other people.	You feel comfortable being by yourself or with others; you see yourself as being able to rely on others and reliable.
You worry that if a friendship or a romantic relationship ends you may never have another.	When friendships or romantic relationships end, you bounce back quickly without giving much thought to why they ended.	When friendships or romantic relationships do end, you are disappointed and wonder why, but know it is probably nothing that you did.

Hopefully you find these examples of attachment styles helpful. For a more thorough and accurate assessment of your attachment style, you should consider taking an attachment test by Dr. Amir Levine and Rachel Heller, authors of the book *Attached: The New Science of Adult Attachment and How It Can Help You Find—and Keep—Love* (www.attachedthebook.com). Research on attachment styles as they exist in adulthood, especially as it relates to friendships, is relatively new and ongoing. The limited research that does exist reports that, with increased therapeutic assistance and some other strategies, such as practicing mindfulness, self-compassion, and re-parenting ourselves (giving yourself the love and care that you may not have received from your parents), our earliest childhood attachment injuries can grow into secure attachments. This is good news if your current attachment style is a barrier to making and keeping friends!

Securing Those Insecure Attachments: Security Priming

Therapy is often a good place to start addressing how your attachment style is impacting your ability to make and sustain friendships, but if you aren't ready to take that step, there is something you can do on your own—it's called security priming. Security priming is easy and, once you learn these strategies, you'll probably notice that you've already engaged in this practice at one point or another.

Consider those word association games that you played in a long car ride or at a sleepover when you were a child—where one person would shout out a word and everyone else would share a related word. It is how marketing works. Advertisers know how to manipulate us into buying things all the time! We are first exposed to a stimulus, whether it is a word, sound, smell, taste, or behavior, that either consciously or unconsciously provokes strong feelings within us. As a result of the stimulus and the associations our brain makes, we are compelled to purchase what is marketed to us. Essentially, security priming is just this, but as it relates to reducing the impact of one's insecure attachments. The goal of this tactic is to prime your brain for friendship-related associations, so you will be well-equipped to move forward in making and keep friends.

Examples of security priming include thinking about words associated with friendship, such as hug, touch, affection, etc., or thinking about times when you've felt strong care, companionship, or nurturing from a friend.[33, 34] The research indicates that those who start thinking about the effects

33   Omri Gillath, Emre Selcuk, and Phillip R. Shaver, "Moving Toward a Secure Attachment Style: Can Repeated Security Priming Help?" *Social and Personality Psychology Compass* 2, no. 4 (2008): 1615-66, https://doi.org/10.1111/j.1751-9004 .2008.00120.x.

34   Manuela Oehler and Elia Psouni, "Partner in Prime? Effects of Repeated Mobile Security Priming on Attachment Security and Perceived Stress in Daily Life," accessed July 08, 2019, https://www.tandfonline.com/doi/full/10.1080/14616 734.2018.1517811.

or the feelings around friendship may be able to overcome the attachment issues that are in their way.

Quick Tip:
Ways to Prime Yourself

Priming is a key concept in modern psychology. Priming can be used to help us elicit positive feelings around certain stimuli. For security priming, the goal is to elicit positive and secure feelings around relationships, including friendships. Mantras can security prime you with positive feelings around a certain situation or event. Here are some quotes/mantras on friendship that may help you:

"The only way to have a friend is to be one."
  —Ralph Waldo Emerson

"In a friend you find a second self."
  —Isabella Norton

"Insecurity kills more dreams than failure ever will."
  —Suzy Kassem

Can you think of a mantra that would help prepare you for a social situation or when you are struggling in a relationship?

HERE TO MAKE FRIENDS

Security Priming

While the research on priming to help friendships is still in its beginning stages, it has been found to mitigate some of the stress faced by those with insecure attachments. Thinking of words, pictures, or memories of being supported has been found to improve mood, self-perceptions, and setting realistic expectations for relationships.[35]

Can you think back to a time when you felt a friend supported you? If so, write it down.

_____

_____

_____

_____

_____

_____

---

35 Manuela Oehler and Elia Psouni, "Partner in Prime? Effects of Repeated Mobile Security Priming on Attachment Security and Perceived Stress in Daily Life," accessed July 08, 2019, https://www.tandfonline.com/doi/full/10.1080/14616 734.2018.1517811.

How does this memory make you feel? Would this be a helpful thought to carry on into your friendship journey?

_____

_____

_____

_____

_____

_____

Write down at least 10 words that you associate with friendship. Look at these words or keep them in a place where you can reflect on them frequently.

1. _____

2. _____

3. _____

4. _____

5. _____

6. _____

7. _____

8. _____

9. _____

10. _____

Introversion vs. Extroversion

The first time I was introduced to the concept of introversion and extroversion was when I took the Myers-Briggs personality type test at my college career center. The goal of taking this personality test was to help determine the types of jobs that would be the best fit for me. After my friends and I took this test we compared notes for weeks—are you an ISTJ (introversion, sensing, thinking, judgment) person or an ENFJ (extroversion, intuition, feeling, judgment) person? While there is much more to the Myers-Briggs personality test than this book has time to discuss, one of the main things the test assesses for is introversion or extroversion.

In college we joked that introverts like to study and are shy, and extroverts like to party and are sociable. Obviously, our college humor failed to capture the nuanced differences in the two meanings. Let's get real, no one prefers to study, right? Jokes aside, the true definitions of introversion and extroversion stem from Swiss psychoanalyst Carl Jung, who defined introverts as those who prefer to focus their energy on their inner worlds as opposed to extroverts, who get their energy from the outer world. From Carl Jung's perspective, both personality types were perceived as healthy and normal.[36] It does take all kinds—introverts, extroverts, and ambiverts (someone who falls in the middle of the introvert/extrovert continuum)—to make the world go around!

Quick Tip: Am I an Introvert, Extrovert, or Ambivert?

No two personalities are the same. However, psychologists who have studied personality types have found that most people fall along the spectrum of either being more introverted or extroverted. If you feel that you are equally introverted and extroverted, you may consider yourself an ambivert.

Introverts tend to be listeners and get energy from being alone, whereas extroverts tend to be talkers and gain energy from other people. Introverts tend to find it hard to trust people and have a few close friends, while extroverts are more likely to be open and trusting of others. The ambivert personality is adaptable. An ambivert can engage in loud conversation at a party but

36 Peter Geyer, "Extraversion-Introversion: What C. G. Jung Meant and How Contemporaries Responded," *Conference Paper: AUSApt National Conference*, October 2012.

also values their alone time. Ambiverts are also good listeners and tend to be very empathetic.

Making Friends as an Introvert

We know that making friends takes energy, and if you are like any introverted person I know, sometimes even thinking about socializing is exhausting. Maybe you're that person who gets an invite but decides to pass because, let's get real, there's nothing more enticing than having some peaceful alone time on a Saturday night. Maybe you're the type who secretly lets out a sigh of relief because drinks with the girls got canceled and you will not be forced to come up with small talk to fill up any silence. It makes you happy to know that instead you'll get the night in to curl up with the book you've been meaning to finish, or binge-watch the latest Netflix show.

The dilemma for introverts is balancing the need to recharge alone while maintaining friendships. Time and time again, I hear stories of how an introvert struggles with staying in contact with their friends, as it requires that difficult mental work of small talk. For introverts, small talk is big work on top of whatever busy schedules they have going—work, family, etc. Many introverts simply feel like they just don't have time (or energy) to socialize with close friends, let alone meet new ones. As a result, if you are on the more introverted side, it's important to focus on those three to five people within your innermost circle, and to do the work to keep those connections close. You already prefer having a small number of close friends rather than a wider net of casual ones. So, it's only right that you take care of those few but meaningful relationships!

The challenge for introverts becomes more complex when work is brought into the picture. Unless you are lucky enough to have a job that provides you opportunities to process and reflect on your feelings, you probably feel exhausted at the end of the workday. Having to go out for drinks after a 9-to-5 day can sometimes be too much. Frequently, the introvert takes on some characteristics of the extrovert just to get by at work or when they're out in public, which can be complicated and confusing. Take the case of Jenny, who was born in a small community where there weren't many people. Growing up there gave her the opportunity for a lot of alone time and less frequent occasions to socialize. This was what she preferred. After college she moved to a large city where she knew no one. Jenny would schedule Facetime calls with her hometown friends, but these calls didn't satisfy the longing she felt for that intimate in-person connection. Jenny took the steps mentioned in this book and put herself out there. She joined sports leagues, said yes to invitations, etc. However, after many months of doing this, she became irritable and simply burnt out. While she had more connections than she thought she would ever have, she was struggling with managing them. Jenny felt conflicted. She knew she needed more alone time to recharge, but felt pressure to keep meeting people. Jenny's struggle is representative of the struggle of many introverts. In public Jenny came across as super extroverted, but the truth was that she wasn't. Over time, Jenny started to take more time for herself to recharge—she scheduled two nights a week to be completely alone. When an extroverted friend would call for a simple quick chat—which can seem like nothing for the extrovert but overwhelming for the introvert—she would schedule a phone date with them for a later time. Sure, this approach was foreign to some of Jenny's new friends, but it helped her identify those individuals whom she wanted to keep close.

Quick Tip:
Combating the Small Talk Scaries

It's the age-old question: How can you muster up enough courage and energy to engage in that annoying small talk? It is a tiring fact of life, and you must do it at one point or another, especially if you are here to make friends! Coming up with a list of things to talk about can make it easier.

Think about good openers. Some examples are:

"What brings you here?" Presuming you are out and about while meeting people.

"What's the best restaurant/food in your neighborhood?"

"How do you like to spend your time?"

"Tell me about your work? What's your favorite part? What do you like the least?"

"Where did you grow up? How did you spend your summers?"

"Do you have any vacation plans coming up? If so, tell me about them."

"What Netflix show are you currently binging? I just finished watching..."

"Where did you go for college?" If you have or know someone in common don't be afraid to share!

Consider practicing these go-to questions beforehand in a mirror. I know that it sounds cheesy, but it can help. Practicing allows you to develop the muscle memory to perform when you need to.

Think about getting out of your head more. Many introverts get stuck in their head and get more used to having conversations with themselves than with other people. Try to start saying what is on your mind with those you feel close to. While it may not be perfect initially, once you start to get the hang of it, you will be able to converse more freely and on an impromptu basis as needed with others. Practice this with others, and ask them how you're doing!

When you get stuck—compliment, compliment, compliment! This strategy never fails if you find yourself stuck in awkward moments of silence. To move the conversation forward, offer up a compliment, then shift. An example may look like this, "Hey, I really like your shoes. Where'd you get them? I might need a pair for my next adventure, which is…" You get my point.

When in doubt, look to make connections among the group. For instance, you may want to try to remember one or two important details about the people you'll be interacting with, and share them with others. Say you are at a work event meeting new people and have just learned something about this new person (where they live, where they went to college, where they work, etc.). Consider sharing this information with the other newcomers to the group, thereby starting a conversation.

Maybe you are like Jenny, an extrovert by day, introvert by night who would rather stay at home than go out and is overwhelmed by too much social stimulation. Or maybe you are the shy person at the party who leaves early and is grateful when the small talk is over. No matter what type of introvert you are, making friends is as important as it is hard. Here are 10 key strategies for making new friends while maintaining the old ones:

1. Ask your friends to market you. If you are an introvert, you don't like small talk, and talking about yourself is even tougher. Why not turn to your closest friends for help? They are already familiar with your introverted tendencies (like how you screen your calls or maybe go off the grid for a few days to recharge), and will likely know who you'll be able to click with and who simply won't understand your social quirks. If you're at a party with a close friend, let them guide the conversation or introduce you to others.

2. Know your limits, and let others know. Set realistic expectations for yourself and own them. Show others your truth and let them accept it (or not). If each social interaction, especially in large crowds, sends your nervous system into overdrive, it is okay to take breaks from social situations and leave early. It's okay to decline invitations to wild parties where you know you'd be unhappy. But try to come up with a new plan with the person who invited you. That way you'll still be putting in the work the relationship needs, but will stay true to what makes you feel good and comfortable.

3. Supplement the in-person time with text/email. You would rather ditch the small talk and get to the point. You want conversations with friends to be close and intimate; however, you may not have the energy or be in the mood to meet up or chat on the phone. The best way to combat this and to let your friends know that you are thinking about them is to text or email. This allows you to stay connected with your friends on your own time, and lets them know you care.

4. Schedule friend dates. The introverts I know need to warm up to the idea of engaging in a social interaction. They may need to psych themselves up for mundane small talk or even come up with a list of talking points before an encounter. Accomplishing these tasks is hard to do on the spot, but becomes easier when planned. By scheduling a phone conversation or a friend date, you are taking control of the situation and everything is on your terms. Plus, you'll have a few days to prepare yourself mentally.

5. Seek out people like you. Since you tend to be a listener, you are more likely to be a target for that chatty extrovert who dominates the conversation. Try scanning the social scene for another introverted person. This may be the person at the party who's quietly standing off to the side, or the person who simply nods and smiles during group conversations. Being aware of those social cues will help you identify other people like yourself. So next time you are at a training session, work happy hour, or other event, check out the landscape. Maybe there's someone sitting by themselves or looking a little aloof that you could see yourself approaching.

6. Join a class. Lots of the literature on friend-finding includes recommendations to join a class or a club. Joining a class may be intimidating, especially if there is pressure to talk or interact with your peers. Being in a new social situation can be nerve-wracking and tiring on its own. A good compromise is to join a class where you will be meeting other people like you. Consider the case of Ruben, a young man in his early twenties who was very introverted. Ruben wanted to make connections but found the basic getting-to-know-you conversations mundane and cumbersome. He decided to pursue a course in philosophy. In class, Ruben met several new people with whom he had an automatic common interest. Ruben was able to have meaningful, thoughtful, fulfilling conversations without having to engage in the nuances of first introductions.

7. Fine-tune those listening skills, and try to talk. Introverts are the best listeners out there, but sometimes their tendency to over-listen prevents them from engaging in the dialogue. Talking for shy folks is tough, but reflective listening may empower you to master both the listening and the talking at the same time. Reflective listening is a communication skill aimed at understanding the speaker's idea and then sharing that idea back to the speaker. By practicing reflective listening, you enable the speaker to feel heard and understood, which often makes both people in the conversation feel good!

8. Buddy up with an extrovert. This is a common pairing for obvious reasons. If you are the introvert in this case, it is probably easy, and maybe even validating, to befriend an extrovert. The truth is that in this scenario you probably don't have to do much work. While this union is positive for many people, I have some words of caution. First, know your extroverted companion well. Are they able to sit in silence with you? Do they always have to be doing something or be surrounded by others? Are they accepting of your tendencies, such as when you opt out of social events? If they can accept you, then it seems like it is a good fit!

9. Don't take things personally. This is perhaps the most important and difficult piece of advice to follow. If you are introverted, you may have just a few close relationships that you deeply value. However, as we all know, sometimes good things come to an end, or something you think will start doesn't. The key here is to not take it personally. Don't beat yourself up over things that might go wrong in the process of making friends; just move on.

10. Practice makes perfect. I am always impressed by self-proclaimed introverts who, over time, comment about how much easier it is to engage with people (small talk included) after years of practice. In fact, I am always surprised when someone who presents as highly extroverted proclaims that in fact they prefer and need to have their alone time to recharge. You might be asking how they were able to do this—through practicing the balance of alone time versus socializing time.

Making Friends as an Extrovert

A common misconception is that introverts are the only ones who struggle with socializing and making friends. While more media attention is dedicated to the needs and challenges of introverts to make and keep friends, extroverts also have their obstacles. We know that, if you tend to be on the more extroverted side, you are more outgoing and get energy and solace from being around people. You are more likely to start up a conversation with someone and knock first friend dates out of the park, but what does it *actually* take for an extrovert to make deep, meaningful connections? Well, it takes work. For extroverts it's important to slow down, to be conscientious, and to be emotionally vulnerable.

The truth is that, while extroverts may feel rejuvenated after being with people, they can also be shy. The stereotypical image of an extrovert is someone loud, the life of the party who can keep going and going. However, if you are like any extrovert that I know, this stereotype is far from true. Yes, they like to talk. Yes, sitting in quiet is harder for a true extrovert than an introvert or an ambivert. But it does take work for extroverts to build emotionally intimate relationships with others.

Have you ever watched an extrovert in action? They can be very good at superficial small talk and conversations. It's not that they like small talk any more or less than the classic introvert, they just can't tolerate the silence. As a result, it is more common for extroverts to have many acquaintances who know just enough about them, but less common for them to have several people within their innermost circle. Additionally, the extrovert may have issues filtering what they say. They go too fast and maybe too far with their talking, and may not always censor what they are saying. This can sometimes create friction within friendships.

Another challenge for the extrovert is taking time for themselves and balancing their multiple relationships. An extrovert doesn't need to be out and about 24/7, tending to their social networks. Like introverts, they also need some alone time to relax and rejuvenate, but they just need less. This can be challenging for someone who is insecure in their friendships and feels that, if they are not actively managing them, they will lose them. Establishing quality connections means investing time in them, which can be a dilemma for the extrovert focused on keeping many acquaintances instead of investing in a few deep, meaningful relationships.

Consider the case of Brian, a twenty-something in New York City. Brian was very socially active and often the life of the party. However, after years of cultivating many acquaintances and friends, he found himself at a loss when they started moving away or getting married. While there would always be more people in Brian's social network, he began to feel lonely and disconnected, as he never really took the time to build a few core intimate friendships.

Unfortunately, Brian's situation is not uncommon and serves to remind us that even those people who may seem to have it all in the friendship department may not be experiencing many friendships of the good. If you can relate to Brian's situation, don't worry! With some self-reflection and mindfulness you can start to build those friendships of the good right now. Here are some strategies for building closer and more meaningful relationships:

1. Take inventory. Research indicates that most friendships last an average of seven years and that for friendships to last longer, they need to be regularly nurtured.[37] Reflect on each tier of your social circles, including closest friends, close friends, and friendly acquaintances. Whom would you want in your innermost circle? What would you need to do to get to know them more? Are you spending a lot of time with people but finding yourself uncommitted to

---

37 ScienceDaily, "Half of Your Friends Lost in Seven Years, Social Network Study Finds," May 27, 2009, https://www.sciencedaily.com/releases/2009/05/090527111907.htm.

HERE TO MAKE FRIENDS

developing the friendship? If this is the case, you may want to spend your energy investing in other friendships.

2. Practice sitting in the discomfort of silence. Sitting in silence, especially in social situations, can be awkward and unnatural. Most people, introverts and extroverts alike, feel the need to "fix it" to ease the discomfort. Unfortunately, this tends to lead to unimportant or superficial conversation. Do your best to make meaningful conversations with those you want to get to know better by keeping yourself from saying something just to say something. A good way to practice fighting this compulsion is to spend time in the same space with a friend, a loved one, or a relative, and let there be awkward moments of silence.

3. Don't badger your introverted friend. You are bound to have more than a few introverted friends. They may not always want to talk to you, go out with you, or meet your new best friend. Though radio silence might make you think they are mad at you, they aren't! They are just quiet. They may not respond right away to your texts, and you may need to accept this in order to keep up the friendship.

4. Practice self-reflection. Extroverts have the tendency to go fast. When you're moving from social event to social event, it's hard to find the time to tune into yourself. Consider taking on a meditation practice to develop more self-awareness. The more in touch you are with your feelings, the more you will be able to develop an emotional connection with your friends. In addition, more self-reflection will eventually lead to improved self-awareness, which will help you develop appropriate coping skills to manage life's emotional challenges.

5. Make quality time count. If you are the typical extrovert, you want every social interaction to be very social. Maybe brunch plans for two evolves into a lazy afternoon for five. The truth is that, if you want to develop closer, more intimate friendships, you have to make quality time count. This means that you have to make room in your busy social life for one-on-one time. This may be hard for some extroverts, as it means having those non-superficial conversations—you know, the conversations that are deep and meaningful. Also, work to respect the need of those close friends who may not want brunch plans to blow up.

6. Listen and stop talking about yourself. As you probably know by now, listening is a key ingredient in bonding with new and old friends, but it is hard for everyone. If you are the introvert, you get stuck in your head, and if you are the extrovert, you probably share too much about yourself. Neither is good for building connections or letting people really get to know you. Consider how you come across to others. If you do overshare, what is it that you say? How do you think this comes across to new people? Take the temperature of burgeoning new friendships by asking more of those intimate questions instead of focusing on your stuff. Try implementing those reflective listening skills (see page 122). If you are struggling to get a sense of how you come across to others, seek out someone you trust and ask for their feedback.

7. Don't take things personally. Meeting new people can be likened to a high, but it can come with some downsides. Have you ever been at a party where you met someone and talked for a few minutes, then knew their name, the college they went to, and where they live? You felt like you had just met a forever friend, but the next time you saw them they walked right past you without even acknowledging you? Going unnoticed if you are an extrovert can sting, but you cannot let it impact you. Yes, the connection at the party you had was real and it felt positive, and that's not to say the other person didn't have the same feelings, but not everyone may be as attuned to people you are!

8. Tell people when you are down. Talking to people when you are down or at a low is a practice in vulnerability and a way to build real friends. It is unlikely that many people even see this side of you (even the life of the party can feel down). In fact, it may be out of character for you to share these feelings, as there is often a lot of pressure on the extrovert to be the outgoing, happy one. Nonetheless, if you take a risk and share, you may be able to identify those friendships worth keeping.

9. Take time to learn how to be alone. Practicing how to be alone is an exercise in self-discovery. As an extrovert, you may never want to be alone and, although you may do everything possible not to be alone, sometimes things are out of your control. Learning how to be by yourself allows you to reflect on what you value in your friendships, providing insight on which ones to develop. Additionally, the more you know and are comfortable with who you are, the more you will get from close relationships. Some ideas for taking time to be alone include going to dinner by yourself, waking up early to enjoy a cup of coffee while watching the sunrise, going for a solo walk, touring a museum by yourself, or taking in a late afternoon movie.

10. Do a friendship check. Far too few do this, but everyone should. Although assessing the state of your friendships with others may seem scary and threatening, if you approach it with the proper mindset, you might just get the feedback you are looking for. I often see young, extroverted adults asking their friends if they are doing a good enough job. While many of us have the same thoughts, those that go out on a limb and ask find themselves armed with some good information. I once tried this experiment with a close friend and it was instrumental in changing the way we communicate.

Quick Tip:
Practicing Gratitude

We all know that being recognized feels good, whether it's from your boss, your coworker, or your spouse. Have you ever considered the impact that expressing gratitude has on your friendships? It can make close relationships closer, create bonds between people, and make one feel understood. Think back to a time when you were really struggling and a friend showed up for you in a big way. How did you acknowledge your friend's efforts? Some research suggests that the more prosocial or helping behaviors between friends are acknowledged, the more inclined we are to be helpful in the future.[38] Expressing gratitude in friendship builds trust and attunement.

The Friendship Common Denominator: Vulnerability

Whether you are an introvert, extrovert, or somewhere in between, one of the main ingredients in any relationship is allowing yourself to be vulnerable. Within the past several

---

38 Yuan Guo, "The Influence of Social Support on the Prosocial Behavior of College Students: The Mediating Effect Based on Interpersonal Trust," *English Language Teaching* 10, no. 12 (August 2017): p. 158, https://doi.org/10.5539/elt.v10n12p158.

years, the concept of vulnerability has become more widely understood and acknowledged as a key component in developing emotional closeness. Although therapists and counselors have discussed this concept on their couches for years, the concept of being vulnerable has become more mainstream thanks to social work researcher Brené Brown.

Brené Brown states that vulnerability is uncertainty, risk, and emotional exposure. She puts forth that vulnerability "is at the core of all emotions and feelings,"[39] and she couldn't be more correct. If you want to connect to people and *really* get to know them, you must let them in to your innermost circle. Not only your innermost friend circle, but into the core of *your inner* self, meaning your heart and soul. This statement may sound cliché or cheesy, but for most of us, it sounds terrifying. Because we have been conditioned to protect our hearts and souls from being rejected, we are not open to vulnerability.

To better understand the concept of vulnerability and the need for it in any relationship, I like to reflect on a commonly used metaphor—that of an armored warrior draped in plates of metal. A metal helmet protects the warrior's head, with only a slit for the eyes and nose, and his hands and feet are protected by metal gloves and boots, a shield, and a sword. This armor is meant to prevent anything from

---

39 Brené Brown, *Daring Greatly: How the Courage to Be Vulnerable Transforms the Way We Live, Love, Parent, and Lead* (London: Penguin Life, 2015), 33.

HERE TO MAKE FRIENDS

penetrating to his core. Should penetration occur, the warrior may die. We tend to put on metaphorical armor when it comes time to show weakness or vulnerability. Consider why the common pleasantry, "How are you doing?" normally gets answered by "fine" or "good." The reality is that a more truthful answer might be more complex and emotional than a simple *fine* or *good*. But we have internalized the idea that showing vulnerability or our true selves is a risk and, moreover, a turnoff to others.

Showing vulnerability is tricky. As I've learned in my work as a relational therapist, it is against our human nature to expose our true, vulnerable, feeling self, first. It makes sense, as doing so comes with the risk of rejection, shame, and abandonment if what we are trying to share doesn't land well with the people we care about. To protect ourselves we end up playing a mind game of "I will only share my vulnerability with you if you show me yours first." It takes a courageous person to show their vulnerability first and, in my opinion, this is why a lot of potential relationships, romantic and platonic, fail right from the start.

I am reminded of one of my own recent experiences when someone was courageous enough to take the first step. I had met this person casually nearly five years ago and, like any good millennial, Facebook-friended them. After five years of liking their pictures, this person, who is bicoastal, reached out to me and had the courage to share that they would like to get to know me better, because they wanted to see what a friendship would look like. I was floored—this had never happened to me. How could I not embrace a gesture like this? This person had shown me their vulnerability first, no way I was going to reject it!

Now that you really understand the importance of vulnerability in developing human connections, are you ready to challenge yourself to be more vulnerable? If so, you should continue reading and be hopeful about the future friends that you will make as a result of your courage. If you are not yet ready to take this most important step in your friendship journey, you should stop reading right now. You may need more time for self-reflection. I highly recommend watching any Ted Talk by Brené Brown or reading her book on vulnerability and the human condition, *Daring Greatly: How the Courage to Be Vulnerable Transforms the Way We Live, Love, Parent, and Lead.*

Quick Tip:
Core Ingredients in Being Vulnerable

As a relational therapist, I've found that the most successful platonic and romantic relationships are those where emotional intimacy is fostered. Individual core beliefs necessary to vulnerability include:

- **Self-worth:** If you believe that you are worthy of love and connection from others, you will allow yourself to be vulnerable.

- **Heart:** If you really want something, go for it. Allow your heart to give and receive love.

- **Courage:** Without courage, you will not be open to the opportunities that love and connection offer.

- **A growth mindset:** Stop seeing things from a fixed perspective and instead examine what could happen if you were more open.

- **The willingness to be uncomfortable:** This is where growth happens. Sometimes being vulnerable means not knowing or being able to change or fix something, which for most of us is against our nature. If you stick with it, you might be pleasantly surprised!

EXERCISE 3.5

Explore Your Beliefs About Vulnerability

If you have made it to this paragraph, you have decided that you are up to the challenge of learning how to be vulnerable. You are about to scratch the surface of developing a new friend-making skill. The first step in building this skill is to explore your beliefs about vulnerability. How we think about vulnerability and how the messages we received regarding vulnerability from our families impact our comfort with being vulnerable and our capacity to be courageous.

What does it mean to you to be vulnerable?

_____

_____

_____

_____

What does vulnerability look like in your family?

_____

_____

_____

_____

How was vulnerability discussed in your family?

_____

_____

_____

_____

What does it mean to be vulnerable in relationships?

_____

_____

_____

_____

How did/do you experience your parents or your family being intimate/vulnerable?

_____

_____

_____

_____

In what current or past relationships have you been vulnerable? What was the outcome?

_____

_____

_____

_____

How is vulnerability received in your family or community of origin?

_____

_____

_____

_____

What are your thoughts/judgments about those who are vulnerable?

_____

_____

_____

_____

HERE TO MAKE FRIENDS

Now that you have a sense of the ways that vulnerability has operated in your life, try to deploy your newfound willingness to be vulnerable. This means being strategic. Too often, I hear stories of one person's decision to be vulnerable first ending in disaster. When taking the first step in being vulnerable with someone or sharing an intimate part of yourself, you want to be mindful, slow down, and consider why you want to be vulnerable with this person. We do this often when pursuing a significant other; however, when pursuing friendship, we tend to either take no risk at all or overshare. In *Daring Greatly*, Brené Brown suggests that those who are thinking about being vulnerable ask themselves some important questions, which I've expounded on here:

What am I hoping to get out of this interaction?

_____

_____

_____

_____

How would being vulnerable create connection with this person?

_____

_____

_____

_____

Could there be another reason why I want to share this information (e.g., maybe my desire to share stems from anxiety, boundary issues, etc.)?

_____

_____

_____

_____

Why is this person worthy of my vulnerability?

_____

_____

_____

_____

Why do I want to share this specific information about myself?

_____

_____

_____

_____

Once I share this about myself, it is no longer a private thought in my mind, and I am never going to be able to retract my share. Am I okay with this?

_____

_____

_____

_____

What are the feelings that are going through my body as I am taking this step to be vulnerable?

_____

_____

_____

_____

How am I hoping the person receiving this information will react? What responses could I receive that would hurt my feelings?

_____

_____

_____

_____

How could exposing this vulnerability meet an emotional need? Am I genuinely asking others to meet my emotional needs?

_____

_____

_____

_____

Quick Tip:
Practicing Self-Compassion

If you have taken the leap and are willing to risk being vulnerable, you also need to prepare yourself for the possibility of feeling let down. Consider the ups and downs of courtship; you sometimes put yourself out there only to have your heart broken. Unfortunately, this can also be true of friendships. As my mother used to say, not everyone is another person's cup of tea, meaning that not everyone is a good fit for everyone else. However, developing a reflective practice in self-compassion can be helpful. According to Dr. Kristen Neff, self-compassion has three core components: self-kindness, common humanity, and mindfulness.[40] Examples of the three components are listed below.

- **Self-kindness:** We all have flaws and areas for development. The best medicine is to approach our flaws and misgivings with understanding and warmth. Consider that even though you may not have lived up to your full potential today, tomorrow is another day.

- **Common humanity:** Feeling inadequate and inferior at times is a universal human experience. We all have the same feelings even though we may experience them at different times and to different degrees.

- **Mindfulness:** Self-compassion takes work. Mindfulness means working to stay grounded in the present moment so that you are not taken over by negative feelings or worry. It means working to stay out of that perpetual feedback loop and in the current moment.

---

40 Kristin Neff, *Self-Compassion: The Proven Power of Being Kind to Yourself* (New York: William Morrow, 2015).

Summary

If one thing from this book sticks with you, I hope that it's the significance of vulnerability in every relationship. Moments of vulnerability are present in our professional relationships, intimate partner relationships, and friendships. Think about all the opportunities when you could easily choose not to be vulnerable—at work when you don't know something or at the doctor's when you don't want to share a symptom. The easier choice to not be vulnerable would leave you at risk.

If this speaks to your situation, consider this quote by poet Criss Jami: "To share your weakness is to make yourself vulnerable; to make yourself vulnerable is to show your strength." Remember that you don't have to be vulnerable in some big way for it to make a difference in your life. Your practice in being vulnerable can be small and gradual; it does not mean loudly spilling your life's details to everyone. And remember that no one is perfect. We all have our stuff and, no matter what yours is, find comfort in getting to know other people's stuff if and only if you can allow yourself to be open to your own vulnerability.

CHAPTER 4

YOUR ROAD MAP TO FRIENDSHIP

The past several chapters have helped you identify the types of friendships you currently have—friendships of the good, utility, and pleasure—as well as your personality type—introvert or extrovert. You've also learned how your personality type impacts the way you go about making friends, and you've discovered some key strategies to help you overcome your personal challenges when making friends. Additionally, you now have a better understanding of the role that vulnerability plays in making and keeping friendships. With the self-reflection that you have done, the aim of this section is to put it all into motion by identifying a clearer road map for friend-finding, -making, and -keeping.

Friendship Inventory

Before we move forward, review your notes from the first few sections of this book. Keep stock of those friends who are in your three innermost circles—those closest to you, your close acquaintances, and those you would invite to a party (or be comfortable with at someone else's party). If this is difficult for you to do, do not worry. I have a strategy for how you can handle this following the next exercise.

Rate Your Top 20 Friendships

Complete the grid on page 148. List your top 20 friends on the left-hand side of the grid and rate your relationship with them according to each category on a scale of 1 to 10, with 1 being the lowest and 10 being the highest. If there is not enough room, feel free to expand this chart on another sheet of paper.

Now, circle the friends and those categories that you rated a 5 and below. For example, perhaps you rated your friend Jane a five and below for positive feelings/relative happiness and intimacy categories. Based upon this assessment, it seems that you should work on developing these areas of friendship with Jane. Of course, one of the first questions you need to consider is how your behavior contributes to your ratings. For instance, maybe you aren't being vulnerable enough or maybe you haven't spent a lot of time one on one with Jane to really get a sense of how reliable or trusting she is. Remember that relationships are reciprocal, and you should not only consider your friend's behavior in the scaling assessment, but also your own.

If these low scores have absolutely nothing to do with you, then you may want to consider if this relationship is worth keeping. Eliminating a friendship where all the scores fall below five makes more sense than eliminating a friendship of 10 years because of a few low ratings. However, you should also consider your values and the aspects of friendship that are the most important to you. When in doubt, make a pros and cons list for the relationship in question. Remember that sometimes friendships (especially friendships of utility) can move around within our three innermost circles. Rating Jane a 3 on intimacy today doesn't mean that in a few months you'd still rate her a 3. Our capacity to connect and care for others is influenced by what is going on in our own lives. Maybe you're currently struggling with having more than a couple intimate friendships, but later in the year you'll be in a better headspace to do so. When looking back on your scale, you'll need to decide if you should cut Jane some slack!

Friend's Name	Friendship Duration (in years)	Positive Feelings/Relative Happiness
1.		
2.		
3.		
4.		
5.		
6.		
7.		
8.		
9		
10.		
11.		
12.		
13.		
14.		
15.		
16.		
17.		
18.		
19.		
20.		

HERE TO MAKE FRIENDS

Reliability/ Trust	Reciprocity	Intimacy	Companionship	Helpfulness

Count yourself lucky if you have a handful of relationships consistently rated a 5 or higher. These friendships are important and special! When you evaluate those high-rated friendships and it seems that they are going well, your focus should be on working to maintain these relationships rather than developing them. Finding the balance is where a lot of people get stuck. It gets even more difficult if, like me, you want to simultaneously work on developing other, less highly rated friendships.

Simple strategies for maintaining your positive, long-standing relationships include regularly checking in, even if it is a simple "I'm thinking about you" or "Hey, how are you? I miss you!" Another way to maintain the connection while working on your other relationships is to express gratitude. There's nothing better than a random text, card, or even email just thanking your good friends for being there.

If you had difficulty filling out the friendship inventory, don't worry. You are like most of us! It is hard to assess friendship, especially when it comes those people in our outermost circles. This just means that you are at a different point on the friendship journey, and no two people or situations are the same. For the friendships that you were able to assess, circle the names of those friends who had the lowest average scores. Write those names on a list. Then write down the names of the other friends on a separate list.

Let's use the example of Jane again. You would put Jane on the lower scoring list, and those friends who scored higher on the other list. For the first list with Jane, you will want to further develop that friendship using the strategies discussed earlier in the book. For instance, you may want to work on building more intimacy with Jane by starting to be more vulnerable. You could do this by sharing more about yourself or asking your friend more intimate, personal questions about themselves. If you are more introverted, you may want to take control of organizing and planning events for you and your friends on a smaller scale so you have control over the situation and create an environment that allows you to be more vulnerable. Your goal should be to raise the ratings of these friendships.

For the list with your high-scoring friends, you will want to maintain those relationships and potentially use those friendships as a launching point for other relationships. Meeting friends through friends is a great way to expand your social circles. We will discuss this more in the following sections.

Quick Tip:
How to Keep Your Close Friends Closer

If you are reading this book, you are probably hoping to expand your network of friends, which is a great goal to have for yourself. But keep in mind that it should not come at the cost of your existing friends. Finding time to connect with your old friends while putting in the time (and energy) to making new ones is a tricky balance. If you are open to the practice of vulnerability, one way to balance these two goals is to talk to your close friends about how you want to make new ones. This gives your friends the opportunity to be supportive and recognize that, while you may be spending more time developing new relationships with others, they too are important.

Your existing friends might help introduce you to people like yourself. Additionally, don't assume that they are always busy. Remind yourself that even when you are busy, you still like getting the invite—I bet your friends do too! In the event that they are busy, plan something with them in the future and make sure it's on both of your calendars!

Setting Your Friendship Goals for the Road Ahead

After completing the friendship inventory, you should have a sense of how to move forward in your friendship journey. The results of your friendship inventory may indicate that you need to: 1) work toward building a variety of new friendships, 2) maintain and strengthen the friendships you have, or 3) weed out those toxic and superfluous friendships so as to build more intimate friendships. No matter what your starting point, it is important to set yourself up for success with goal setting.

You probably remember the importance of goal setting from school, or perhaps you set some goals as you prepared to enter the workforce. But how often do you employ those strategies today? The truth is that most people typically don't even consider setting goals for relationships. When looking for an intimate partner, they typically think it is enough to date a lot or until they have found someone who checks all the boxes. In a friendship, you may apply a similar tactic: hang out with as many people as you can, build out your online social network, and wham—you have friends. Wrong. To build and sustain friendships, you need to approach them like any other goal in your life—you probably aren't going to a run a marathon without training and expect to cross the finish line. Even in your friendship journey, you will have to set some goals for yourself.

Let's start with a brief review of how to set goals using the SMART goals acronym. Goals need to be:

- **Specific:** Clearly define your goal. Depending on the outcome of your friendship inventory, you should have a specific goal: attain more friends, strengthen and maintain friendships, and/or eliminate unhealthy friendships.

- **Measurable:** Determine how you will measure your goal before starting out. In this instance, friendships can be measured in quantity or quality. You might want to make five new friends in a year. Having something quantifiable allows you to measure your progress.

- **Achievable:** Set realistic and attainable goals. This is perhaps the most important component of goal setting. I get it, you might want to have a gazillion close, intimate friendships, but how realistic is that? Many people have goals that are not realistically achievable, and then they are hugely disappointed when they fail. Unlike other goals, friendships are not entirely in your control, so it is even more important to set realistic goals for yourself. Remember the helpful mantra "The slower you go, the more progress you make!"

- **Relevant:** Align with your goal. If you wish to develop closer, more intimate relationships, then your goals should reflect this. For instance, if you were to amass 20 new friends and not develop intimate connections with them, this would not be aligned with your goal.

- **Timely:** Set a time limit for your goal. This is where most goals fail. Think about the common New Year's resolution to lose weight. How many times have you heard of someone saying that they were going to lose five pounds or go to the gym, and after a month, they have stopped watching their weight and forgotten about the gym? Although this may be hard to conceptualize as it relates to friendship, you may need to set a time limit for your specific goal.

If your goal is to increase your number of friends or develop more quality relationships, this will take time. I recommend having several goals. You might start with your overarching, long-term goal. This may be to increase your social network to 12 people. You can then break that broader, long-term goal down into several smaller goals. The risk of starting off with a broader goal is that you may lose motivation when you don't see results quickly. If you can set up and achieve smaller goals, you feel more positive and more motivated to keep working toward your larger goal. Since setting goals to make friends can be particularly challenging if you suffer from introversion or social anxiety, starting small also helps to keep the process from being overwhelming.

Quick Tip: Keep Your Goals Actionable

If you are like me, you probably find yourself biting off more than you can chew. This is one of the key challenges in goal setting, and it happens to folks trying to expand and grow their friendships.

Take the case of Kai. Kai had spent most of his young adulthood working and not enough time playing. By the time Kai was 30 years old, he wanted to expand his social circle. Luckily, Kai didn't have to date, as he had a partner, but he realized that over time he had let his social network disintegrate. This made Kai feel depressed. Not only did he lack a solid social network, but having been out of practice, he had also developed slight social anxiety.

When we started to work on Kai's Friendship Goal Map, he had high hopes: going out for drinks a few times a week, group workout plans, hiking, etc. Indeed, his goals sounded exciting, but they were too ambitious! After a week of all this action, Kai was ready to give up. We had to lower his high expectations for a booming social life to more manageable ones. Instead of aiming for the whole shebang, Kai lowered the bar. Together in therapy, we worked on his fear of being judged by others. When Kai would start to think about how he would be received by others, he noticed that his heart would start to race and his palms would get sweaty. He was super worried about saying something that would be perceived as weird or silly. The focus of our work was not only to address his social anxiety, but to also address how his expectations of himself were not necessarily aligned with reality. We worked to help him employ not just positive thinking, but also realistic thinking.

Kai wasn't the type of person to randomly act inappropriately or in a foolish way, so his fears that he would weren't based in reality. After some cognitive behavioral work, Kai was able to shift the way he thought about himself and started to feel better about the idea of engaging with his colleagues. For the first few weeks, he aimed to go slow and participate in one social activity of his liking a week. Over the next few weeks, he upped this number to two social activities and eventually capped out at three social activities a week. Kai was also mindful to take control of these outings when he could. By asking some old pals for coffee or drinks instead of them arranging the social outing, he was able to mentally prepare. Kai's experience is a good reminder of the risk of burnout, especially if being social is newer for you or if it has been a while.

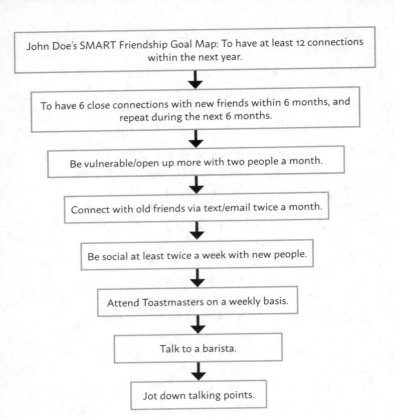

John Doe's SMART Friendship Goal Map: To have at least 12 connections within the next year.

To have 6 close connections with new friends within 6 months, and repeat during the next 6 months.

Be vulnerable/open up more with two people a month.

Connect with old friends via text/email twice a month.

Be social at least twice a week with new people.

Attend Toastmasters on a weekly basis.

Talk to a barista.

Jot down talking points.

Look at John Doe's SMART Friendship Goal Map above. Let's assume John Doe suffers from some challenges in the friend-finding and -keeping department because of social anxiety, introversion, or difficulty in being vulnerable with others. John Doe is using his SMART Friendship Goal Map to achieve his goal of developing 12 closer connections in the next year. John Doe's smart goal may look like this:

HERE TO MAKE FRIENDS

John will develop 12 close connections over the next year by further developing friendships with six people in the next six months. He will be able to do this by allowing himself to be more vulnerable and taking risks to speak to people outside of his comfort zone, such as the local barista. Consider what your own SMART Friendship Goal Map would look like by completing one for yourself below.

Remember that this is just a sample of what someone's goal map may look like. We all have different goals and situations that factor into how fast or slow we can accomplish them. Critical to achieving your goals is writing them down. Too few people write down their goals and, as a result, fail to achieve them. After all, it is easier to ignore your goals when they are just floating around inside your head. If you write them down, they become real.

Could you imagine crafting your own Friendship Goal Map? Could you imagine placing your Friendship Goal Map someplace you can readily see? Try this exercise on your own. Don't be afraid to break your large goal down into as many small goals as needed.

Create Your SMART Friendship Goal Map

The aim of this exercise is to identify several smaller goals that are in the service of your larger friendship goal. You don't need too many smaller goals; I recommend starting with four or five. If you have more, feel free to add them.

Coming up with the smaller goals, or pit stops as I like to call them, on your friendship journey can be difficult. Consider those annoyingly long car trips that you took with your family as a kid. Maybe the driver didn't want to take any pit stops along the way, making the ride that much more unpleasant. However, if you were lucky enough to have a driver who was willing to entertain pit stops, the interesting experiences you had along your way made it easier to get to your destination. Think of the smaller goals as the pit stops on your longer journey!

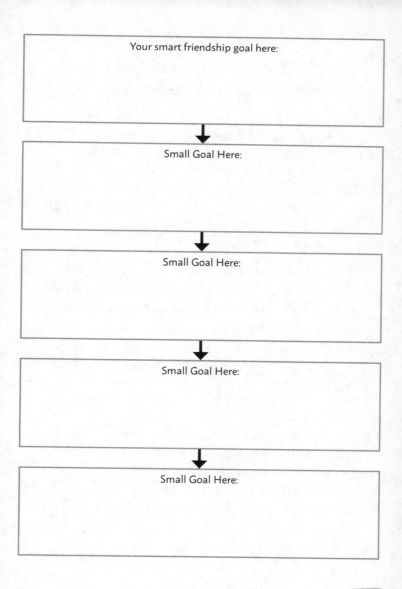

Your smart friendship goal here:

Small Goal Here:

Small Goal Here:

Small Goal Here:

Small Goal Here:

Quick Tip:
Always Negotiate and
Renegotiate Your Goals

When setting goals, you need to constantly negotiate and renegotiate. We all know that failure is part of success, but have you ever stopped to wonder why? Even in the best-case scenarios when we are thoughtful about our large goals and strategical about our smaller goals, we run the risk of failure. Failure, as you may have heard, is part of the human condition, and without it there would not be any success.

That said, sometimes SMART goals aren't enough— because they aren't entirely dependent on or controlled by you. Take the example of John Doe. He wants to have 12 new connections in 12 months. Sounds perfectly reasonable, right? Maybe it is if he follows through with all of his smaller goals and no other confounding factors get in his way. But he's human and those connections he hopes to make are also human, meaning that a number of barriers to this goal will likely get in his way. This is okay and to be expected. John Doe can reassess and renegotiate his goal. Maybe making 12 close connections isn't possible in 12 months because of work schedules or family obligations. Maybe 10 new close connections is a more feasible number.

Those who do not stop, reassess, and renegotiate their goals are at risk for not completing them. Remember that just because you need to adjust or amend your larger goal does not mean you won't get there—just don't stop!

Summary

There's a short- and a long-term game at play when making lifelong friends. Unfortunately, it is not as simple as it was when we had more time and less responsibility. Using your road map and staying mindful of your emotional and physical capacity for this journey is key. The great thing about goals is that you can always reevaluate and readjust them as needed. Just don't give up on them because you're scared of failure!

By taking small steps in your journey, you will be able to mark and celebrate your gains. Even the smallest gains, such as jotting down points for small talk, should be acknowledged and celebrated. The more you honor even your smallest achievements, the more likely you are to stay on track and motivated. Remember, making friends is a process. Whenever you get caught up in impatient or negative thoughts, consider the saying, "it's a marathon, not a sprint." If you hurry through life, you'll miss things.

CHAPTER 5

MAKING CONNECTIONS

Now that you are armed with your road map and have a sense of your starting point—whether you are working to find new friends, maintain the old ones, or eliminate some toxic friendships—you can start your journey. The best part is, no matter your starting point, you don't need to start from scratch. You might have doubts about this, especially if you've moved to a new city and are having trouble meeting new folks, but it's true. With social media and technology doing the networking for us, we are even more connected to "people who know people." When talking about our own interpersonal connections, we're likely closer than six degrees of separation!

Examine Your Networks

For some, the following recommendations seem like common sense; for others they may be intimidating, but don't worry. The first step in making friends, especially if you are struggling, is to examine your current social networks. Review the exercises that asked you to list those you are in contact with and those you would like to be in contact with. Ask yourself if there is any connection between the people you already know and have a rapport with and those you would like to get to know better. Would you ever consider asking an established friend to connect you to a potential friend? Think of it like networking or an informational interview for a job. It's not a big deal if the connection doesn't pan out, and at least you can say you tried.

Within our existing networks, we may have people who are really, really good at connecting people. In *The Tipping Point*, Malcolm Gladwell talks about three different archetypes of people: mavens, salespeople, and connectors. Gladwell considers mavens to be information brokers, those people who openly share what they know to others, and salespeople to be those individuals who are incredibly persuasive and can garner support behind them. For the purposes of this book, we are going to focus on connectors. Although Gladwell emphasized the ways these archetypes promote change, his theory about connectors within social networks applies to how we can make friends. He describes connectors as natural hubs for human resources. If you ask them a question, without thinking, they will recommend someone who knows someone. Connectors are active in our workplace; you just need to assess who these people are in your social networks. You may be able to identify them, as they tend to be more extroverted, love engaging with others, and are able to zoom in to any situation and identify the perfect person for you. Consider that old childhood neighbor who is always eager to set you up with their son/daughter/friend's son or daughter. Could these people be connectors? You bet!

Interestingly, Gladwell suggests that it is not necessarily our close inner networks (close friends and family) who are the most helpful in building connections, but those acquaintances found within our outer networks. His premise is that the people we meet randomly at a social or work gathering might be more useful to us than those people who know us more. On one hand, this makes sense. Think of the friends you have—you likely spend your free time doing similar things and with the same people. As a result, there's not a lot of room for new and different people. Those in our outer networks bring forth their different networks, as a result allowing for more access to others. Consider the next time you are at party and find yourself talking with someone new. You may want to show curiosity about who they know. Mention an activity or sport you enjoy and that you are looking for some new companions. I wouldn't be surprised if they tried to set you up with someone they know right there.

Now the question is: How do you find those super-connectors in your network? While we all have connectors in our networks, consider seeking out those super-connectors, or people in your network who are especially good at not only networking and putting people in touch, but who use their connections to build communities out of their networks. Super-connectors are geniuses at not only knowing who's in the know, but also fostering authentic relationships with those they know. We know that not all people fall into this archetype, and we wouldn't want to assume that just because someone is chatty and friendly they are the gatekeeper to our future friendships. Keith Ferrazzi, the author of *Never Eat Alone and Other Secrets to Success, One Relationship at a Time*, suggests that the best way to find super-connectors is to identify them by their fields of work.[41] For instance, acquaint yourself with people in professions that engage and connect with others. In theory, if you can connect with people like this, they will in turn introduce you to new people. Some of the key connectors to look out for include restaurateurs, publicists, fundraisers, headhunters, and those involved in politics. Other possible super-connectors are those who work in media, Instagram influencers, the local bartender/barista,

---

41   Keith Ferrazzi, "Connecting with Connectors," Inc.com, March 01, 2005, https://www.inc.com/resources/sales/articles/20050301/connections.html.

the PTA president, that person who works from home (or an office share environment like WeWork), attorneys, and salespeople.

You might be thinking: So how do I use this information in my own personal life, and what do I do with it? First, do you happen to have any close friends on your friendship inventory list who have any of the above-mentioned careers? If so, start with them. Ask them if they know of anyone in their network who has interests similar to yours. Would they mind setting up an introduction?

Understandably, it may feel uncomfortable at first to ask this of your network, especially if it is small. However, you have to start somewhere, and the first step is often the scariest. Don't forget that we have all been in this place at one time or another. Alternatively, you could pursue the larger networks in your world. If you start going to the same coffee shop for a quick break at lunch or have a drink at the same bar, you'll become a regular. Eventually, the staff will start to recognize you, and conversations will blossom. You will probably meet other regulars as well. Often I hear stories about how someone got a job or an invite to a backyard BBQ simply by going to the same place in the community over and over.

Consider the case of KC, an immigrant who moved to a small town outside of Boston. KC didn't know anyone and was simultaneously looking for a job. KC went to the same coffee shop every day until one day, another person approached them. Long story short, KC ended up chatting with this person, who was a connector. Not only did KC develop a long standing friendship with that person, but they ended up getting a pretty good job through this person's contacts. Friendship is often at the heart of professional opportunities, so when it comes out of nowhere, it's best to accept it!

Quick Tip:
Try Being a Super-Connector

At first glance, this sounds intimidating, but it's easier than you think. As we get older, we look for opportunities to connect, step out of our routine, and do interesting things. If you are the ultimate introvert, you may not *always* want to do something new, but you may want a new experience from time to time.

One way to be a super-connector is to host a gathering. It doesn't have to be big. Whether it is a formal party or a backyard BBQ, maximize your opportunity to connect with others by having your invitees bring one person you don't already know. Trust me, they will be eager to do this, and my guess is that a number of your invitees want the very same thing as you—to meet new and interesting people. This way, it will be up to your guests to introduce you to new people (less pressure on you to make small talk with people you don't know), and you can feel more at ease since you already know the majority of people at your party.

Acting as a connector yourself, even if you are shy, can be easy if you are in your area of expertise. Perhaps you are the quiet type who would rather code than sit at a bar and have a drink with an acquaintance. That's fine, but play to your strengths. An expo or a meet-up in your area of expertise might allow you to feel more in your comfort zone, where you'll be able to meet new people without the pressure of nonsensical small talk, because you will already have a nuanced understanding of the topic at hand.

Take the case of Zane, a former client in his early twenties, who worked overtime most nights and did not leave the office much. Zane was very good at talking shop, but not very strong in talking about anything else. It was hard for Zane to connect with people outside his industry, and at work he and his colleagues were too busy too fraternize. As an alternative, Zane went to a local business meet-up that he found on meetup.com where he was able to socialize and make some long-standing professional and personal connections.

Map Your Connectors

This exercise will help you identify and map out possible connectors in your life. Use the findings from your friendship inventory. Also consider other networks in your life, such as work, family, alumni organizations, and affinity groups to identify potential connectors. Remember that your best connectors may not be those within your innermost circle, so think a little bit more broadly. Complete the following lists and circle those you are most likely to ask for connection recommendations.

Close friends who are potential connectors:

1. _____

2. _____

3. _____

4. _____

5. _____

Acquaintances who are potential connectors:

1. _____

2. _____

3. _____

4. _____

5. _____

Community members/institutions who are potential connectors:

1. _____

2. _____

3. _____

4. _____

5. _____

Now that you have identified connectors, take the next step and list the top three people whose names you circled. These are the individuals you would most likely reach out to and ask for some support in meeting people like you.

Top three connectors:

1. _____

2. _____

3. _____

Feel free to list as many individuals as you can beyond the top three potential connectors. The more, the better!

Now, focus on what that first conversation with these connectors might look like. Obviously, if you have a preexisting relationship, your initial conversation will likely be easier than with someone you don't know at all or don't know that well. For the purposes of this book, focus on developing an initial conversation with someone you don't know well. The hope is that by practicing these types of conversations in advance you will feel less nervous. See the below narrative as an example.

John Doe: "Hi, Jane. It's nice to talk to you again, and thanks for agreeing to meet up with me."

Jane Doe: "Of course, John, not a problem. How are things going? What have you been up to?"

John Doe: "Lots going on with work and living in a new city. Things are going pretty good, but I am adjusting to the work-life balance."

Jane Doe: "It can be hard."

John Doe: "Yes, it can. I'm curious, how did you first manage it when you moved here and were transitioning from college to the workforce? It's kind of hard to rebuild a social network with work and everything."

Jane Doe: "It is hard, I had to make a lot of effort—connecting with alumni organizations and going to happy hours. How do you like to spend your free time?"

John Doe: "Ideally, I would like to find a new group of people to shoot some hoops with on the weekends. Know anyone who is into that?"

Jane Doe: "I'm sure I do. I know lots of people. Let me put out some feelers. Maybe I can organize drinks with a few people in the next few weeks. What do you think?"

John Doe: "That would be great, Jane. Thanks."

Can you imagine how you might approach an initial conversation? Write down some of your thoughts, and try not to put too much pressure on yourself. Use the space below to brainstorm your first conversation with one of your top three potential connectors.

_____

_____

_____

_____

_____

_____

_____

Helpful Hints for a Great First Impression

When you meet that connector and get that long-awaited introduction, it is important to put your best foot forward. We all know that first impressions are meaningful. Don't stress too much, but consider these helpful hints when preparing for your first encounter with a connection.

1. Have a current event in mind to speak about, if appropriate. Be mindful that not everyone will be want to discuss politics or religion, but it is always helpful to tune in to the news beforehand. Alternatively, being in tune with pop culture can also make for casual and easy conversation.

2. Prepare and practice conversations geared toward the person with whom you are speaking. People always love to talk about themselves, and this is the easy part. Perhaps you can start by asking them questions about some of your shared common interests.

3. If you are feeling stuck, don't worry. Remember to use that reflective listening skill discussed earlier in the book. Worst-case scenario, repeat the last few words that they said in an uncertain voice—think about how you can use your tone in a questioning manner to imply that you are asking for clarification. Many times, this will encourage the other person to continue their train of thought, allowing you to focus on listening.

4. Have some go-to entertaining stories to share. When you are trying to relate to someone, it is always helpful if you can provide an entertaining narrative around that experience. People are always engaged by those who are good storytellers, but the reality is that this takes practice. It is always helpful to have four or five go-to stories before networking. Practice telling these stories as frequently as possible in as many ways as possible. Practicing in front of a mirror is always helpful and allows you to experience your own performance. I notice that when I change my tone or use inflections in my storytelling, people become more engaged with my narrative.

5. Be mindful of the person before you. Mirroring or modeling somebody's body language can be very helpful, especially if you are both on the quieter side. Body language is another form of communication and you want to pay attention to other people's body language cues. While you may be preparing yourself for a grand performance, it may not be necessary if the person before is you is on the quieter side. In fact, if you are too over the top or boisterous, this can be a huge turnoff.

6. Have intentional and purposeful conversation. While intentionality is not needed in true friendships, it is a key ingredient when getting to know someone. An aimless conversation could risk losing the attention of your audience. Instead, have some goals for that conversation. One goal might be to meet up again and, if you hit it off, you may want to plant that seed before you say goodbye!

7. The most important piece of advice, no matter what, is to follow up. Perhaps your first meeting didn't live up to your expectations, but don't let that discourage you. First meetings can be intimidating not only for you, but also the other person.

Finding a super-connector or being the connector are two ways to help you reach out and attract some prospective new friends, but there are other, more proactive ways to achieve a similar goal. Consider being part of a larger community, as mentioned earlier in the book. We start to find friends when we are younger via school and our communities and, later, through our children's school communities, if you have them. Don't forget that community is everywhere, you just may not always know where.

Examine Your Communities

Think about some of the things you are interested in, such as running, fishing, fashion, or reading. Where are the microcommunities focused around these things within your local community? Book clubs are a great place to acquire potential friends because they provide an opportunity to engage on a casual basis. You do most of the heavy lifting by reading the book yourself, and there's not a lot of pressure to have deep, insightful opinions. Book club members recount how the afternoon typically deviates from the topic at hand to more personal topics—a prime opportunity for burgeoning friendships.

Exercise communities are also terrific places to meet others without a great deal of pressure. If you have ever been in the gym long enough, you'll notice that there is a diverse body of patrons and some downtime between sets or weightlifting. People milling around are very curious about what others are doing. Such opportunities can be golden because 1) you can engage in casual conversation as the workout gives you fodder for conversation and 2) there is no expectation for you to commit to a detailed conversation, as everyone there knows that you have a greater purpose and likely the next round of exercise to get to.

Another community that is very welcoming and receptive to newcomers, even if you aren't athletic, is the running community. Many municipalities have running clubs for new and more seasoned runners. Even if you don't decide to join a club but participate in a few races, there are often some good pre- and post-race events for all to participate in.

If you are not the most athletically inclined, consider trying a new class or volunteering. The key here is to seize opportunities where people are organized around one common interest. Many communities have online forums or bulletins that list volunteer opportunities or classes. The best part of volunteering or trying a new class is that it can lead to other opportunities. Time and time again, volunteering proves to be a great opportunity for folks to meet other people. I often hear from those who click with someone after one day of volunteering, and then plan to do another volunteering event with them in the future. The hope is that over time these connections continue to grow, and your volunteer buddy will blossom into a friendship.

If you like someone, ask them to exchange their contact information with you in case a similar volunteering opportunity comes along, or if you are classmates, ask for their number in case you miss a class. Consider sitting next to that person during class or asking them for a coffee afterward. Text your volunteering buddy the next time a similar volunteer opportunity comes along and invite them!

While you don't always have to start from scratch, sometimes you may have no other alternative. Maybe you recently moved to a new city and learned that your existing networks have no connections where you now live. Creating your own connections can be easy with the right mindset. New places, like new opportunities, allow you to foster a new you. Perhaps in college, you were introverted and shy. However, in a new place, the prospect of meeting new people is an opportunity to reinvent yourself. Consider putting yourself out there and introducing yourself to your neighbor. Or, if that is too bold, just say "hi" and make small talk in the elevator—make it even easier on yourself by simply asking them what they think about the building. Who knows, you may get an out-of-the blue invite to go hang out!

Quick Tip: Reinventing Yourself

The concept of reinvention has been around forever. Think of the people who lost it all then miraculously made a great comeback: Martha Stewart, Robert Downey Junior, Arnold Schwarzenegger. While it is true that these celebrities may have reinvented themselves in the service of their careers, they remind us that it is never too late for us.

You've probably reinvented yourself many times before—think back to the first time you went to sleep-away camp, started a new school, or decided that you were going to be a different "you" when the new school semester started. We each have multiple parts of our personalities that we decide to share or not share depending on who's around us. For instance, you may be bubbly and outspoken with one group of people and a bit shier and quieter around another. Your opportunities to reinvent the way you are around people or on social media are endless. Consider the following steps:

- Examine how you think others think of you, how you see yourself, and how you would like to be perceived. Is there a gap between these three perspectives? If so, how might you narrow the space?

- Explore your strengths and areas for development. Once you have identified them, write them down.

Making Connections

Strategize ways to grow these areas. Accept that during periods of growth you will be uncomfortable.

- Practice ways to share your new self-image with others. Consider sharing a new perspective, image, or value to your existing network. This could be a photo of yourself being the new you (e.g., if you have never worked out before, maybe post a photo of yourself working out on Instagram. Or share a favorite quote or a book that is representative of the "new you.").

- Try new things that align with your new self-concept.

- Seek out support and encouragement. Ask your supporters to provide positive feedback and reinforcement when you need it.

- Fake it until you make it. We have all had impostor syndrome at one point, but over time, if you are confident, optimistic, and brave enough, you will get there, I promise!

Summary

Networks are all around us, but to tap into them you need to be on the lookout for them. Super-connectors are always doing this. Shifting your mindset even just a little to be more like a connector will help you see and utilize possible networks. Interestingly, while connectors are great at connecting other people, they sometimes struggle to connect with others outside of their intimate circle on a deeper level. A common complaint of connectors is that they are never introduced to their friends' social circles. If this applies to you, remember that reciprocity is a key ingredient in friendships.

If you are starting from scratch, be daring and put yourself out there. Try new experiences. Seek out opportunities and social activities where there will be people who have similar interests to yours. Just remember to have compassion for yourself if some of these opportunities don't work out. Sometimes you can chalk it up to timing or not being a good fit. I promise if you keep trying it will work out. Don't take it personally, you will find your people! For more suggestions on places to meet new people, check out the Appendix starting on page 238.

CHAPTER 6

PLAYING THE DIGITAL FIELD

In many ways the advent of social media has leveled the playing field for all types of relationships: professional, romantic, and social. Before, if you were on the introverted side, dating and friend-finding was much more difficult. Now, with social media, we can take risks without much at stake by reaching out and "poking" others.

Additionally, for better or worse, social media allows us all to be more vulnerable. We are often inundated with glossy selfies and vacation pictures that intentionally make other people's lives look *amazing*. In our parents' generation, few people outside of the family were likely to ever peek at those family pictures. This access to much more of people's intimate lives automatically allows for vulnerability. On Facebook and Instagram, we could learn of the death of someone's close family member even though we are far removed from the person.

Consider the sense of familiarity that online dating enables. After chatting for just a little while, you know enough about that person that a first date can seem more like a second or a third. Socializing online, if it works, accelerates relationships, which has its pros and cons.

We're all busy, and sometimes meeting people online is just easier. While I fully believe meeting people in person is the only way to fully assess true chemistry, online socializing can help those who struggle with first-time introductions and small talk. Consider how much easier it is to swipe right than it is to get ready to go out on a first date!

Friend-Finding on Social Media

Friend-finding on social media is much like dating. Top considerations are compatibility and chemistry, though the chemistry part is very different from the chemistry that exists between intimate partners. Nonetheless, as with online dating, you must be careful not to fall into the vortex that is social media—too much liking, swiping, and tagging can lead to aimless consumption of media without any gain. It is important to approach it with intentionality. Remind yourself what it is you are looking for in a friend, and keep a written or mental checklist while you are scouring

Instagram, Bumble BFF, or other outlets. Remember that, because there is less at stake in using social media, you may be compelled to like someone for the sake of getting more likes.

Social media platforms that aren't designed specifically for making friends can still be used to that end, because many adult friendships are based on commonalities. Take Instagram, for instance. Start by identifying one to three interests—such as crafting, fitness, or dog ownership—that you would be interested in building friendships around. Using Instagram's search functionality, you can enter keywords (for example, "crossfit" or "newyorkcrossfit") associated with those interests to pull up related hashtags and accounts. Looking through those accounts, you may come across people engaged in the activities you love to do. Pay attention to whether or not they geotag their posts. That way you might find, for example, a CrossFit gym in your area with a community of like-minded people, or learn about a training session or lecture open to the public. Consider going to that gym to try it out for yourself. Make it a goal to speak with at least one person while you're there. One way to do this is to be up front about your new-ness while asking about the gym's community, culture, and values. To participate in the community more actively, post images of yourself practicing your passion (for example, take video of a few seconds of your latest CrossFit work-out), and tag your location, a few keywords, and maybe even your coach, if you have one. This can become a way for you to communicate with teachers and influencers you value. In this way, you can organically grow your network of fellow enthusiasts around your passion, and you just might find that by putting positive energy out there, some of those enthusiasts become friends.

Another simple strategy: Make a habit of commenting on other people's posts (existing friends or accounts you enjoy) or responding to their stories from time to time. People enjoy positive attention, and it's one way to stay top of mind and connected. People are more likely to think of you as they plan get-togethers, and if you want to suggest grabbing a coffee or meeting up, you'll have laid the groundwork. This applies to Instagram, but also to Facebook and other social media platforms.

Friend-Finding Checklist

It is easy to get sucked in to the vortex that is online friend-finding. This exercise aims to redirect your efforts with intentionality. Review the work that you have done in the past several chapters. Take into consideration the types of friendship you want to have in your life—friendships of the good, utility, and pleasure. Think about the core values you want in a friendship. When searching online for prospective new friends, keep this checklist in mind.

Write down the top 10 qualities or values you are looking for in a friend.

1. _____   6. _____

2. _____   7. _____

3. _____   8. _____

4. _____   9. _____

5. _____   10. _____

Now circle your top three values. Ask yourself how you will know if someone shares these values. What will you be looking for in their social media profiles?

Friendship No-Gos

Knowing what you are looking for in any relationship, especially in friendship, is important, and so is knowing what you don't want. For instance, if you are really into hiking and camping, you may buddy up with someone who has similar interests instead of wasting energy on someone who doesn't like the outdoors. For some, social media is used as a self-promotion opportunity and may not offer the prospective of new friends. So consider your friendship no-gos or deal-breakers ahead of time. Write down the top three friendship deal-breakers for prospective new friendships (e.g., smoking/non-smoking, indoor type/outdoor type, drinking/no-drinking, reader of great literature/tabloid news, Boston fan/New York fan. You get my point).

1. _____

2. _____

3. _____

Armed with these lists of must-haves and deal-breakers, you will be well-equipped to narrow down your online friendship search. Like dating, you can sift and sort through many profiles, but try to limit your time doing so. This can be done by creating small goals for yourself. Once you have found 10 people you like, work to reach out to a few of them. Remember that, if your real goal is to make quality friendships, you must reserve energy and time to really get to know people intimately.

Set Parameters

Setting parameters around the time spent on social media and the number of social media outlets you are using will also be helpful. One complaint that I have heard about online dating is that it can feel like being a kid in a candy shop with so many options. In my experience, the folks who say this are perpetual daters who are struggling to commit. Failure to commit also happens in friend-finding. For some, using social media platforms to find friends allows more access to more people, which can discourage focusing on a few prospective friends and developing deeper relationships with them. Remember that time is of the essence and don't get carried away with all the options and lose track of your main goal—finding good, quality friends.

Reach Out First

Consider the effort you put into online dating to find just ONE person. Depending on your friendship goals, you may not be looking for one person but a few. Once you have found someone you are potentially interested in, you need to jump on it and take some risks. You may have to be the one to initiate conversation, like a post, or even publicly comment on someone else's feed! If someone who sparks your curiosity reaches out to you, respond quickly, but in a meaningful way. No one wants to receive a trite response such as "uh huh" or "ditto."

Build on What You Started

Consider the examples in this book to build engaging conversations. If you dare, start being vulnerable with prospective new friends and ask them about their experiences in making friends online. You will have to be willing to share a little bit about your experiences as well. Some of the best and most meaningful connections come when you open up and share your experiences—people feel more trusting of you, and sharing is a way that you can connect easily with someone new. Moreover, the benefit of using social media to connect with others is that it minimizes the blow of rejection. You may not get the response that you were hoping for, but you just completed the hardest part of friend-finding by putting yourself out there! Plus, there are plenty of other options, so you can keep your search going.

Use Friend-Finding Sites

While finding friends online via social media sounds easier than meeting people in person, there's still work that goes into it. Thankfully there are some supersmart techies out there who have done the hardest part of that for you! Yes, today there are a variety of platforms that use algorithms much like the dating sites to match you up to those with similar interests, personalities, and within a radius that you set.

The goal of these sites is much like the dating apps where you are swiping until you get a match. Unlike other social media platforms, with friend-finding sites you must create your own unique profile and be a very active participant. You are not going to make friends simply by swiping right, and you are also going to need some interesting one-liners. Friend-finding sites like Bumble BFF provide catchy one-liners to help you start engaging, but users indicate that those who are their most authentic selves (i.e., those who are open and authentically sharing why and what they are looking for) have the best results. Here are some popular friend-finding apps.

Atleto. A meeting place for those who are athletically inclined. Need a running buddy or someone to spot you during your Saturday-morning weightlifting session? This app matches athletes with similar interests and skill level who are geographically close.

Bumble BFF. Similar to the Bumble dating app, Bumble BFF helps you identify people in your neighborhood who have similar interests as you. Start up a quick and friendly conversation, and if you feel the chemistry, set up a meet-up! This app sorts potential friends by age, relationship status, and interests using an algorithm. You match with potential friends based your profiles. When using this app, be mindful that the app only gives you a limited time to see your matches before they disappear.

CLIQ. Unlike other friend-finding apps, CLIQ allows you to connect with preexisting social media friends, search for new groups and, if you click, invite them out. The first step in using this app is to identify some topics that you are interested in. Then, based on your interests, the app will send you some "goodies" and recommend places where you can meet up with people. If you vibe with someone, you will be given the option to "huddle," or to chat privately with that person.

Friender. This app connects friends with similar interests. It provides over 100 interests and activities you can select from.

FriendMatch. FriendMatch is a membership-based online matchmaking service that pairs you up with prospective friends. It also provides events for its members.

Peanut. Peanut shows like-minded moms or primary caregivers near you and allows you to swipe left or right depending on the end user's preferences, like hobbies, location, etc. It offers an alternative to Facebook "mom" groups.

Realu. This app is geared to those who have recently made a transition, whether it is a job change, location change, or relationship change, to find platonic friendships that are perfect for you, based upon your interests.

Skout. This friend-finding app is very accessible and has the capacity to connect you to a prospective friend in almost 200 countries. Skout allows you to make social or business contacts, and then chat with them.

Squad. To use this app you need to be a member of Facebook. The goal is to choose five Facebook friends who are part of your "squad." Once you have your squad, you are asked to set a goal for your squad. You are then able to meet and match up with other squads; however, you only have 24 hours to message and make plans. Squad also allows for screensharing, so you and your friends can watch YouTube together, if you choose.

Meet My Dog. The best part of this app is that it isn't just for you, but your dog too! This free, private social network enables you to discover and connect with other dog owners near you. Who doesn't want to share cute photos of Fido while on their friend-finding journey?

We3. A friendship app where you swipe cards about personability, lifestyle, beliefs, and values and are then matched to tribes of three compatible people of the same gender, with similar traits, mutual interests, and goals. By answering a variety of questions aka cards about yourself, the app will build out a profile that helps others know who you are and whom you should connect with.

MeetMe. This app promises to meet the need for human connection by helping you to meet new people within your location who share your interests. MeetMe allows you to join over 100 million people who are interested in video chatting, messaging, and streaming.

Vina. Focused on females, this app allows women wherever they are in the world or in their life's journey to connect with other like-minded women.

Quick Tip:
Your Go-To Friend-Finding Apps

Friend-finding apps are becoming more popular as people realize that finding friends can be just as hard meeting a mate. Some of the apps below cater to a broader audience while some are more specific. Remember that friend-finding on friend apps is not for everyone, and that it is OKAY! You have many more opportunities to meet your people. Don't forget to post pictures and quotes that reflect your authentic self. You want people to swipe you because of who YOU are—the worst is having to engage with someone who is not interested in the real you.

Join an Online Community

Playing the digital field to find and keep friends is more than just joining friendship apps like VINA and Bumble BFF. Joining an online community can also be helpful. A few years ago, some of my rather distant Facebook friends started promoting a new workout and nutritional plan, which then morphed into a community. I was amazed at how groups of people that I never anticipated coming together, came together. In addition to using a more individualized approach to friend-finding, consider joining online communities for meeting potential new friends. If you own a dog, join a pet-related group on Facebook or Instagram, or if you are into running, follow some running blogs or start your own. Just be aware that one of the risks with joining an online community rather than a friend-finding site is becoming a passive participant. If you are sincere about your friend-finding goals, you absolutely do not want to be passive. Instead, be a mindful participant by providing feedback and asking questions. Hopefully your commentary will elicit other's comments and opinions. One helpful hint: People are always receptive to positive feedback and compliments. Check out some of these online communities:

Amino. This app consists of a network of communities that are dedicated to a certain topic. You can chat with other members of your communities by text, voice, or video chat. You can also create polls, blog posts, or wiki entries.

Meetup. This app enables you to join groups within communities who share a certain interest. The best part about this online community is that you can participate in something new or something you already love, all while having an opportunity to meet new and interesting people in person.

Nearify. This app provides daily updates on events in your neighborhood, allowing you to connect with diverse people with similar interests.

Nextdoor. This is an online community about your local community. Check out the latest posts from your neighbors or post something yourself. By participating in this forum, you will never miss another block party or local event.

* * *

Don't forget to take that final leap of faith and make the request to bring the online friendship into real life by extending or accepting opportunities to meet in person. For some online friendships, getting together regularly in person may be limited due to distance. However, it is still important to make a point of meeting in person. For example, one friend group whose members met online but live in different parts of the country take turns reuniting with one another for their annual vacations.

Setting Yourself Up for a Successful First Meeting

Now that you have done the leg work to meet prospective friends (you've connected through social media, chatted a bit, and have a sense of their likes and dislikes), it's time for the scariest part of friend-finding—the long-awaited in-person meeting. Before you break into a sweaty panic attack, remember that this first meeting is probably just as hard for the other person as it is for you.

The first step to a successful first meeting with a new friend is to prepare yourself mentally. Too often we get stuck in our own heads and run through negative scenarios that may arise. If you find yourself doing this, work on some of the thought-stopping techniques discussed earlier in the book. Have a conversation with yourself—yes, I am advocating that you talk to yourself and recount the reasons someone would want to be your friend. Maybe list three to five reasons and recite them periodically to yourself. Over time, you will internalize some of these reasons, and this will boost your confidence.

Practice having conversations with your new friend before you meet them. Being a good conversationalist takes practice. I am not suggesting that you run up to random strangers and start talking, but imagine what you would say. For instance, one of my friends who struggles with social anxiety regularly imagines what he would say and how he would start a conversation with people walking down the street. For some, this practice technique may seem strange, but it seems to be working for my friend. It is always good to have a list of go-to stories or questions for your new friend. Remember that you likely already have something in common with them, so build upon this connection.

Once you are mentally prepared for your first friend encounter, consider where and how the meeting will take place. Obviously, your meeting place will be mutually agreed upon; I also recommend finding a space that is convenient for both of you and an activity where you don't have to commit too much time or feel too much pressure. For instance, you may not want your first meeting to be a six-course dinner spanning five hours, but maybe a quick coffee or a workout activity where you can get to know one another. This strategy is especially helpful for people who are more introverted or shy. Say you and your prospective new friend are interested in rock climbing or anime. Find a local event related to one of those interests that you can participate in.

When engaging with your new friend, be curious and ask open-ended questions. Consider preparing and rehearsing these questions (and their answers) beforehand. While your inclination may be to connect over things you have in common, explore your differences. Be mindful to take an open and nonjudgmental stance. No one likes to engage in a conversation that is critical in tone.

To make good conversation, see the other person in their best light. For instance, when I was on a first friend date, my friend was sharing the difficulty that they were having at work. I made sure to see and recognize their efforts to resolve the situation and acknowledge how talented they seemed at their job. A critical part of engagement is to always make the other person look and feel good. Don't forget to focus on the positives in this initial conversation. It will help keep the conversation going. Also, remember to use reflective listening (see page 122).

The most important part of the engagement process is to absolutely be your authentic self. You can be the best conversationalist and practice this first friend-date encounter as much as you want, but it isn't going to go anywhere unless you are being you. You wouldn't want to waste your time going out on several dates to realize that you aren't dating the person you thought you were, so why would you waste someone else's by being inauthentic? Worst-case scenario you got some extra practice for future first friend dates, and best-case scenario you are one step closer to having a friend within your friendship circle.

How to Be Social On and Offline

If you are out of practice chatting with folks you have just met online or if socializing in general is challenging for you, know that one-word conversations are not going to cut it. Making meaningful conversations on social media can be as difficult as making small talk in person. Socializing online can even be challenging for extroverts, who typically feed off others' energy. Like preparing for in-person small talk, it is also good to have a repertoire of conversation starters for chatting online, such as:

"What's your experience been using this app for making friends?"

"What brings you to [insert name of city/location]?"

"Tell me about your favorite thing to do in the city?"

"What type of adventuring are you into?"

"How do you spend your downtime?"

"What is your favorite food/local restaurant?"

"What are some adjectives your current friends/family would use to describe you?"

Now that you have some examples of conversation starters, write down 5 to 10 conversation starters of your own based on facts that you would be interested in knowing about someone.

1. _____

2. _____

3. _____

4. _____

5. _____

Quick Tip:
Putting Your Best Digital
Self Out There

There's a lot out there about how to start and negotiate online friendships, but not much about how to make your best first impression. Many friendship apps suggest that you put up a few pictures of yourself doing the things that you like to do. This is a great first start. If pictures with other people are an option, post some of those as well so as not to post all selfies—this can be a turnoff and suggest that you are more invested in yourself than others.

Review your goals for friendship and find pictures of yourself that align with those values. Not all your pictures need to be perfect—being too perfect can also be intimidating for some. By showing the true you through photos (e.g., a picture of you being silly), you are allowing yourself to be vulnerable and letting people be attracted to the true you. Choose pictures where you are enjoying the moment—such imagery will make your prospective new friend want to be there with you!

Summary

Perhaps the best part of online friend-finding is that, once you have met those with whom you truly connect, you can still maintain your profiles and participate in online communities for self-expression and identity development. Socializing online can be amazing, but you need to set limits to how much time you spend online. This can be a challenge for some. After all, you do need to invest a fair amount of time to have meaningful connections online. However, save some of that time to actually get out and meet those online friends in person. There's nothing more important than assessing if the friend-chemistry you have over social media stands the test of meeting in person. If you are lucky at finding friendship online, maintaining those connections via social media can be easy and allow you and your newfound friends even more intimate access to each other's lives.

CHAPTER 7

THE ART OF PUTTING YOURSELF OUT THERE

You've found a prospective new friend. Now, you need to take it to the next level. Maybe you met someone online and really clicked with them, or maybe you've been itching to introduce yourself to your next-door neighbor who seems approachable, but the thought of making the first move is terrifying. The truth is that making the first move is the hardest part for ALMOST everyone, but consider how many times you have had to do this in the past and were able to overcome it. When you put this into perspective, doesn't it seem less intimidating?

Consider the case of Lane, who struggled with socializing at his workplace. Lane had been working at his current job for about a year and half. He wanted to break in with the work clique but was very shy and quiet. It had taken him about a year of working at his previous job before gaining the confidence to socialize with his colleagues. When discussing his current dilemma, Lane was reminded that he had experienced the same situation a year before. He had the road map for handling this situation and wasn't even aware. In fact, when recalling the other times that he had to be uncomfortable and put himself out there, he realized that breaking into this group was not all that hard. Within a week of discussing this dilemma, Lane told me that he had mustered up enough courage to accept an invitation to the office happy hour and was feeling more confident in his ability to put himself out there.

Channel Your Self-Esteem

Lane was lucky that he could recall overcoming a past challenge and use that to catapult him forward, but we are not all that lucky. The other day I was walking with a friend when we were approached by a restaurant host. He was super affable and friendly, which makes sense because he wanted our business. Yet, both my friend and I were amazed at the confidence and ease he showed while making conversation. Shortly after this encounter, my friend mentioned that he wished he could have some of the host's self-confidence to boldly put himself out there. I suggested that we try a little experiment. Could my friend imagine what it would be like to be this host for one moment? Could he imagine himself having a level of self-confidence where he could just go up to anyone and start a conversation? We made a bet that if he could channel this lesser-known part of himself with the next person he encountered, I would give him 50 bucks. Maybe it was because of my bet or the fact that imagining this other part of himself helped my friend's self-esteem, but sure enough he put himself out there with the next person he saw. I watched my shy friend start a conversation with another person who was standing in line next to him at the grocery store. I lost my bet, and he gained some self-confidence.

Quick Tip:
How to Casually Put
Yourself Out There

Maybe you aren't that person who can take a major risk and put yourself out there on a whim. Not many people are, and the most challenging part of this is knowing where to start. As someone who is always intrigued by social encounters, I have noticed that those individuals most skilled in this area do a few of the following things. First, if they are interested in making conversation with someone they don't know, they actively seek some commonality that they can use in conversation. For instance, my shy friend started asking questions about the food items a fellow shopper had in front of him. Although nothing major came of this conversation, he challenged himself and started up a random conversation with a stranger.

Another way to find commonality with someone is to follow up with the last thing you heard them say. For example, maybe you are at a party and the last thing you heard was someone talking about their latest vacation to Cancun. You may interject by saying, "Did I hear someone talking about Cancun?"

A third tip is to start off a new conversation by complimenting someone as you approach them. We can all use a compliment, and it is hard to turn someone's advances down after being flattered! If you are going to use this strategy, make sure you have something else prepared to say after you offer the compliment.

Recognizing Past Resilience

We can all empathize with Lane's dilemma of wanting to engage and put himself out there but experiencing some apprehension. As Lane did, we must recognize our own resilience. We have all experienced trepidation, apprehension, or fear and, at some point, overcome it. It is a good practice in self-awareness to recognize your own strength. Below, write down one time when you have had to overcome an obstacle or barrier to putting yourself out there.

The last time I had to put myself out there was when:

_____

_____

_____

_____

_____

_____

_____

Thinking back to this time and knowing that I had the strength and the power to overcome this obstacle, I feel:

_____

_____

_____

_____

How can I remember this experience so that it will help me find the courage and strength to persevere through new and difficult situations?

_____

_____

_____

_____

Now that you are in the process of remembering that you are resilient and that you can put yourself out there, you are probably wondering how. While it takes a large amount of courage to boldly walk up to someone, introduce yourself, and then ask them out on a friend date, there are definitely more subtle ways to do this that might not make the other person feel intimidated (remember, intimidation works for both ways!).

1. Invite your prospective new friend to an activity/event in which you both share an interest. For instance, a friend of mine was interested in meeting new male friends, and he accepted an invitation to a pick-up basketball game with a prospective new friend. In some ways it was ideal because there wasn't too much pressure to connect in an intimate way right away, and any one-on-one social anxiety dissipated as they were active and among other people.

2. Introduce new friends to other people. If you are ready to take a friendship to the next step, consider inviting another prospective friend out to the friend date. Make it low-key—maybe drinks, coffee, brunch, a workout class—and see if the group of you connect. Having a few people meet up, especially if two people already know one another, makes the outing more casual and, for some, less intimidating. The more people are present, the less work you may have to do to keep up the conversation. Also, if the friend date is not going so well, having a wing person there makes it easier to leave early, if desired. Best-case scenario: all three of you can connect again and, worst-case scenario, maybe just two of you will end up having a long-standing connection.

3. Organize an event. This can be something small, maybe with a few people you know (but would like to get to know better). An event has a set time limit and expectations are clear. Examples are a crafting event, an organized wine tasting, or a 5K run. While your main goal is to cultivate friendships of the good, it isn't the end of the world if you end up with more friends of utility or pleasure.

4. Start small and go bigger as you get more confidence. If you are working up the courage to put yourself out there in a big way but are not quite ready to boldly walk up to someone and extend an invitation or introduce yourself, start small. Take advantage of the technology that is available. For instance, if you are organizing an event, you could send an Evite or an email and bcc the other invitees. You could also start a group text (if the others involved already know one another), which will likely reduce the risk of your text being ignored and hopefully start an interesting conversation.

The more you put yourself out there, the easier it is and the more confidence you will have moving forward. Know the times of day when you feel your best. I typically feel my most outgoing during the mornings when I am fresh; however, some people feel less inhibited at nighttime. Know yourself and when you are at your peak, and optimize this opportunity.

Visualize putting yourself out there—whatever that may look like for you. Consider how professional athletes train before a big game. Even Olympic athletes not only train their bodies but, more importantly, train their brains before a performance. By mentally rehearsing what to expect on the field or during the match, athletes can zero in on the moment and the task waiting for them. When that moment comes, these athletes have imagined it hundreds of times. They are able to control their breathing and block out the crowd, allowing themselves to be mentally present in the face of stress and adversity. You might be thinking that applying this concept to your friend-finding efforts is a large leap, but it isn't. In a way, putting yourself out there, especially if you have some anxiety, is like preparing for game day, and you should treat it as such. Try the visualization exercise below.

EXERCISE 7.2

Visualization

As with vision boards, the goal of this exercise is envision yourself making new friends. Visualization, when done right, goes beyond imagining the image of you doing something and uses your other senses to understand what that experience might be like. For visualization to work, it must be done regularly.

Take several deep breaths and close your eyes. Imagine that you are starting a conversation among a group of people you don't know or introducing yourself to someone you don't know. Imagine you are your most confident self. What would you say to this prospective new friend? What questions would you ask? How would you want that person to respond? How would you feel walking away from that conversation?

This is just one example of how you can approach visualization. Visualization is deeply personal, and if this exercise worked for you, you should not let your imagination stop here. Keep on going! Even if this is the only visualization that you ever do, that is okay. It's still helpful to get a sense of what you would like to see happen when putting yourself out there. Like a professional athlete, you may not get the desired outcome, and that is okay if you know you tried your best!

Focus on Nonverbal Communication

People often focus on their verbal communication skills, neglecting their nonverbal communication skills, such as eye contact, posture, and stance. You may be saying all the right things to indicate your interest in building a friendship with someone, but if you appear closed-up or seem unapproachable, you might be sabotaging all your hard work. More often than not, people focus more on the non-verbal communication than what is actually being said.

Now that you have this awareness—that it takes both verbal and nonverbal communication to connect with people—assess what you know about your body language. This can be difficult. Your body language can be confusing for prospective friends.

Take the case of Lydia, who came to therapy because she was struggling to make friends in her new building. Lydia appeared to be working hard to make connections and would send out community emails, organize the building's holiday party, and occasionally have the neighbors over for drinks out on her patio, but she wasn't getting those sustained connections she wanted. From her perspective, Lydia was never on the receiving end of her efforts. One day, a neighbor who was constantly being invited to Lydia's events, remarked about how Lydia never responded to her friendly gestures when she saw Lydia in town. Lydia was shocked by this feedback, but it helped her become aware of the other ways that she was communicating. She was then able to work on being more aware of her surroundings and being less aloof. With some practice on being more present and understanding social cues, Lydia was able to gain and maintain those friendships she wanted.

Not everyone is as fortunate as Lydia to have a bold neighbor give them feedback on their nonverbal communication skills, but sometimes you get feedback from other areas, such as your employer, a lover, or your family. Sometimes cues about your style of communication can be even subtler. Maybe you are like Lydia and notice, that despite your efforts in trying to connect with others, your efforts seem ignored. This is a good opportunity for you to assess your own nonverbal communication skills by trying the exercise below.

Tuning in with Nonverbal Communication

The aim of this exercise is to help you tune in and become more aware of your nonverbal communication. By becoming more aware of the way you approach various situations, you will be able to practice ways to improve these skills. Even if you think you are a very strong verbal communicator, it is important to realize that you are also communicating nonverbally. For this exercise, you may want to elicit the feedback of someone you trust who can help you answer these questions objectively. Circle the answers that apply to you.

1. Do you give eye contact when you speak to a person?   Yes   No

2. Are you often asked to help a stranger with directions or to lend a hand at work?   Yes   No

3. Can people read your emotions on your face?   Yes   No

4. Would people say you are warm?   Yes   No

5. Do you carry yourself in a relaxed manner?   Yes   No

6. Would others say you have a warm, friendly tone?   Yes   No

If your answers were mainly "no," you may benefit from working on your nonverbal communication skills. Remember that nonverbal skills are just as important, if not more important, than your verbal communication skills, because they can convey your emotions and your true intentions. Below are some key ingredients of positive nonverbal communication.

Make and maintain eye contact. A good trick is to always know the eye color of the person in front of you. If you keep this in mind, it allows you to be present in the conversation, but also lets the person you are talking to know that you are actually interested in them. Making and keeping just enough eye contact can be challenging for some. Make sure that it is not overly intense but sufficient for the

HERE TO MAKE FRIENDS

conversation. For those who struggle with maintaining eye contact, practice in small intervals until you can maintain eye contact for minutes at a time.

Engage your countenance. Work those facial muscles so that they mirror the expression and/or emotion of the person you wish to engage. Mirroring expressions is a way to help demonstrate attunement, care, compassion, and validation. Send the message that you care and are interested in the other person.

Watch your tone. Remember when your parent told you to "watch your tone?" Don't we all? If you are like most of us, you had *no idea what the heck they were talking about.* The truth is that we can all get a little snippy now and again, and at times may take it out on our relatives. But sometimes our moods are reflected how we speak. Imagine if you used that tone on someone other than your parent?!

Take a welcoming stand. As a therapist, I see how important postures, gestures, and mannerisms are in conveying a point. In couples therapy, one partner may be stiff as a board with legs and arms crossed while simultaneously confessing their love. Their closed-up body language doesn't match or even make sense given what they are communicating verbally. When engaging with a prospective new friend, one strategy for ensuring that you are giving off welcoming and warm body language is to periodically do a body scan. Notice if you feel tense or stress in your body. If you see that your arms or legs are crossed, readjust. By opening up your body posture, you give off welcoming body language.

Cadence is key. Being mindful of your cadence or how you modulate your voice is another characteristic of a successful nonverbal communicator. In good conversations, there is an easy flow of information. If your cadence is too fast or too slow, that can throw the conversation into a state of awkwardness. If you go too fast, the other person may interpret your communication as too intense or disinterested. If you find yourself speeding up your cadence, don't forget to be curious about the person in front of you.

Now that you have some strategies for fine-tuning your nonverbal skills, you should also pay more attention to how you receive other's nonverbal communications. You are likely not the only person working on this part of themselves. How do you manage a prospective friend whose nonverbal communication doesn't make you feel comfortable? This can be tricky for a variety of reasons, including the risk of losing out on a possible friend and the possibility of hurting their feelings. Before you make any decisions about cutting off a prospective friendship, see if the inconsistency in their words and actions (such as the case with partner in couples counseling) is a chronic issue or just a one-off. All of their nonverbal cues should be considered together as a measure of their overall intentions. If, after some assessment, you still don't trust them, then it may be time for you to put a hold on developing the relationship further.

Learning to Like Yourself

A clichéd notion is that the more you like and love yourself, the more others will like and love you. Think about the people you find attractive. What is it that attracts you to them? Is it their looks? Their popularity? Perhaps. However, I bet that you are also attracted to their apparent self-confidence or how they assert themselves. This may not be true for everyone you meet; but, it's generally true that most of us gravitate toward and admire people who are confident. Think about that funny guy at a party who always makes the best jokes and tells the best stories. We all know a person or two like this, and most people are attracted to this type of individual. Why? Well, it takes a lot of self-confidence to be the center of attention in a way that's not annoying or overbearing.

Liking yourself is no easy feat, especially for those who did not get enough validation during their early years. In order to attract friends and put yourself out there, you need to know what you like about yourself so that others can start to like you. Often, we don't reflect on what traits or characteristics make us likable to others, we just expect them to, well, like us! It can take other people to see the positives that we don't see ourselves. If you've read other self-help books, you probably know about the law of attraction: like attracts like. If you go out into the world appreciating and loving yourself, you will attract people of the same sort. Keep in mind that self-love is not the same thing as self-absorption. Liking yourself helps you to like other people through vulnerability and empathy.

Knowing Why Others Should Like YOU

Knowing that before anyone can be your friend, you must be your own best friend, complete the exercise below, which asks you to reflect on what you like the most about yourself. You may want to keep this list on a separate piece of paper and carry it around with you. When you need a self-esteem boost, pull it out for a refresher. Additionally, you can add to the list whenever someone (anyone) shares what they like about you. Good luck!

10 things I like about myself:

1. _____

2. _____

3. _____

4. _____

5. _____

6. _____

7. _____

8. _____

9. _____

10. _____

Summary

If you have made it this far, it indicates two things: 1) you haven't run for the hills and 2) you have a lot of courage. Putting yourself out there is a risk and, as has been demonstrated throughout this book, if you don't take the risk, you may be alone. The first step is always the hardest and gets you prepared for the next time, and there is always a next time. If it doesn't go as planned, don't forget to practice self-compassion and remember that not everyone is meant *for* everyone and that you will find your people if you keep on working on putting yourself out there. Remind yourself of what you like about yourself and why others should also like those things. Don't forget to treat yourself as you would your own best friend and reflect on what you like about yourself when you are feeling low. This approach will shift your frame of mind when you are challenged in your friend-finding journey. Many times, we approach putting ourselves out there from a very negative place instead of believing that people out there want to meet us!

CHAPTER 8

MAINTAINING AND ELIMINATING FRIENDSHIPS

Once you have found some friends and decided to keep them, you need to figure out a way to maintain them while managing your life and work. While the act of finding friends is hard, maintaining them is harder, especially when your life and theirs are busy. When the focus is on maintaining the relationship, reciprocity is key. I often hear of friendships that end because it's always one person doing the maintaining. In solid relationships, the reciprocity comes easily, whether it's the back-and-forth text messages, the phone calls checking in, or the exchange of invitations. In fact, in Aristotle's friendships of the good, there doesn't need to be a one-to-one ratio of reciprocity, but the understanding that you are there for your friends when they need you, and vice versa.

In my experience, maintaining friendships of pleasure and utility are harder because that deep bond is missing, and sometimes a deep understanding of one another is too. For friends I am emotionally close to who live far away, I can reach out and feel like nothing has changed. In these relationships, even though you and your friends may not have the time, they know when they need to offer it up. When your friend has recently lost a parent, is struggling with feelings of depression, or just really needs a helping hand to move, you have the sense that you need to put your own self-interest aside and step in. You may not be able to step in all the time, but in those friendships that are strong and working, you should know when you need to. For those friendships that are not as quite developed, I find more acts of reciprocity are needed to maintain the connection (i.e., you receive an invite out, then it is your turn to extend an invite next).

Maintaining relationships goes beyond acts of reciprocity to accepting and celebrating your friends' differences and achievements. While we may be similar to our friends in some ways, we don't always think alike and/or value the same things. In order to have a strong friendship and keep it, you need to support what's important to them, even if you personally don't agree. A common example of this is being supportive of a friend when they are experiencing difficulties in the romance department. While you may not agree with their approach or choices, sometimes letting them know that you are on their side has deep meaning and sustains the friendship. The best and most long-standing friendships are those where you always have each other's backs.

Another important skill is making time to effectively listen. Sometimes you may just want to hang with your buddies and zone out, but an important skill is paying attention to what is going on in your friends' lives. Not attending to your friends' needs will catch up to you and can either cost you a long-standing friendship or keep a strong friendship from blossoming. It is critical to foster transparency and honesty in long-standing friendships. Good friends have the ability to be honest with one another while also being compassionate, even when there are conflicts.

Managing Conflict Within a Friendship

Whether you like it or not, conflict is inevitable and, for most of us, uncomfortable part of life. If conflict in your day to day—at work or at home— is hard, conflict with a friend, especially someone that you call upon in times of stress, is awful. Conflict sometimes arises and can make or break even the best friendships. However, this is largely determined by how the conflict is managed. Many people do their best to avoid conflict, but this is not always healthy for you or for the relationship. Conflict in a friendship can help solidify the relationship and sometimes even help the individual grow—as sometimes friends can be our best and worst critics. Here are some strategies to use when managing friendship conflict.

1. Be calm. Being calm in a situation where you feel misunderstood or pained is difficult; however, it is important to collect yourself and have full presence of mind before engaging with a bestie over a difference of opinion. You will want your friend to fully hear your perspective, which is difficult for them if you are very, very upset (think crying/yelling).

2. Be aware of your feelings before you talk about them. Bring awareness to what you are actually feeling. This will help your friend genuinely understand why you are so upset. Before approaching your friend with your feelings, take an inventory of *all* your feelings, as many times we tend to focus on the angry feeling and not the more nuanced, vulnerable feelings such as sadness, disappointment, longing, etc.

3. When you do talk about your feelings, use "I" statements. Once you have deciphered how you really feel about the situation, remember to frame it using statements that use the formula, "I feel/felt [name your feeling] when [name the event/behavior]." Using this language will help your friend understand your vulnerable feelings instead on focusing on how they are going to defend themselves in the conflict. This reduces the risk of the conflict escalating and builds empathy for you.

4. Set the stage. For optimal conflict resolution results, pick an appropriate space, place, and time to address your friendship issues. Be aware that your friend may not see such a conversation coming and might have a strong reaction, especially if this is the first time you are tackling a conflict in this way. Choose a neutral setting if you are meeting in person, and a good time/day to speak if you are talking over the phone. I typically don't recommend texting/DM/emailing for any conflict resolution unless you have done it before and the outcome has been favorable.

5. Repair, repair, repair. A conflict is never truly resolved until a repair or resolution has been made. You may have heard that this is necessary for couples following an argument, but I would argue (no pun intended) that a repair is necessary for any group of people—friends or family—following a conflict to move forward. A repair is when the perspectives of both parties are heard, the conflict at hand has been discussed, and there is a mutual agreement to continue to work on resolving the tension.

6. Seek out conflict counsel. Consider getting a third-party mediator/counselor if your friendship has seen better days, but the two of you are still motivated to work out your issues. Although friendship counseling is not commonplace, it should be as more and more of our friends are becoming our surrogate families and our communities. Friend therapy was particularly helpful for one cohort I worked with who comingled their friendship with their employment. It can and has been done. A good book on how to navigate conflict within existing friendships is *When Friendship Hurts: How to Deal with Friends Who Betray, Abandon, or Wound You,* by Jan Yager.

Signs of Healthy vs. Unhealthy Friendships

Maintaining friendships requires navigating conflicts from neutrality, meaning finding the balance between expressing your own feelings of hurt without acting or sounding judgmental or parental. We all make mistakes and experience mishaps in friendships. When these conflicts or upsets occur in healthy friendships, they are quickly and easily repaired. That said, many people end up trying to repair unhealthy or toxic friendships when they should be discarded.

As is often the case in unhealthy romantic relationships, people fear the absence of friendship/companionship so much that they stay in even the unhealthiest friendships. It can be difficult to determine if you are in a friendship that just needs work or if your friendship is just not working out. As a society, we don't acknowledge unhealthy friendships in the same way that we do unhealthy romances and family relationships. Given that romances and families sometimes do not offer the support that they should, it is even more important to take stock of our friendships and make sure they are good for us. Healthy friendships typically have the following features:

- **Honesty.** It should be a no-brainer that honesty is part of a healthy relationship; but many of us have that one friend who we actually dislike deep down, but we ignore that truth for the sake of avoiding conflict. An indicator of a healthy friendship is that you are not only honest with yourself, but also honest within and about your friendship. Sometimes being honest can be difficult and painful, but it should be the foundation of all true and longstanding friendships.

- **Reciprocity.** Reciprocity is an indicator of a healthy relationship. There needs to be mutuality in the relationship so that it is never one-sided. Sometimes even healthy friendships may feel one-sided—say your bestie needs a little bit more of you following a breakup—but as long as this is not the status-quo and you eventually feel that things have evened out, then you are in a good relationship.

- **Empathy.** You need to need to have an empathic friend if you are going to get that good friend support when you need it. A good friend will be able to empathize with you and understand your perspective.

- **Respect.** Respect is at the core of any healthy friendship or romantic relationship. Respect in friendship does not only mean deeply admiring your friend's qualities and capabilities but also their boundaries. Respect for friendship boundaries may mean respecting other relationships and/or friendships or even your friend's opinions.

- **Resolution of conflict.** For friendship to be healthy and long-standing, both parties need to do a good job at managing conflicts, as they are bound to happen. Friendship conflicts that end in a repair are happier and last longer.

Understanding and Getting Rid of Toxic Friendships

In all relationships—romances, family relationships, and friendships—we experience highs and lows along with a myriad of other emotions ranging from happiness to disappointment, jealousy, and anger. In each of these situations, we need to decide how much of these adverse feelings we can deal with before we decide that these relationships are bad enough that we no longer want to be in them. Earlier in this book, we discussed the components that are essential to develop long-standing friendships, including reciprocity, interdependence, and emotional intimacy. What happens in moments of betrayal or when you learn that one of your closest friends has talked about you behind your back? Or if they have sabotaged another burgeoning friendship that you were invested in? Deciding when a relationship is too bad to stay in rather too good to leave can be excruciating, especially when the fear of loneliness, hurt, and disappointment await.

Friends cannot and will not be good friends all the time; it is important to weigh the costs and benefits of the friendship before deciding to eliminate it from your life. Explore what you are getting out of the relationship compared to what you are losing (in some cases, trust or self-respect). You may find that you are the one doing all the emotional heavy lifting, and this needs to be carefully considered as well. Friendships take time and energy to make and maintain, and if they are riddled with conflict and are costing you your emotional and mental well-being, they may not be healthy for you.

Knowing the signs of unhealthy toxic relationships is difficult, as each relationship and person is different. So, what are the telltale signs of unhealthy friendships? See some indicators below:

It shifts from feeling good to feeling bad all the time. You used to enjoy spending time with your friend as you were getting to know one another, but lately it just doesn't feel good.

There's always conflict. You feel like you are always working to resolve some sort of issue or are overly accommodating to appease your friend. Your emotional needs and wants come second.

Promises are often broken with little regard for your feelings. You notice that your friend makes promises but when it comes time to make good on them, they bail. You are left feeling annoyed and rejected with little to no explanation.

Jealousy starts to rear its head. You realize that you cannot spend time with others except your friend, and if you do spend time with others you know that you may be headed toward a fight.

Trust issues arise. You used to think your bestie had your back, but maybe you heard some rumors about your friend badmouthing you or not standing up for you. Maybe your bestie is starting to show romantic feelings for your significant other. You are not sure if the person you were once friends with is the same person today.

They only show up when they need something. When you need them, they are AWOL. Unfortunately, we have all had friends like this—you know, the ones who call or text you without even asking how you are doing. They then spill about everything in their life, and an hour later they are too busy to ask you about yourself and need to jump off the phone.

They never take responsibility for their actions or apologize. We all make mistakes and sometimes hurt other people's feelings, even those people we love. Friendship is about give and take and owning up to when you are wrong. Good friendship allows for conflict to happen and the repair to follow.

They are emotionally abusive and mean. Good friends should be rooting for you and have your back. They should shower you with words of encouragement and positivity. There is no room for emotional abuse in any relationship.

It turns too competitive. The admiration the two of you had for one another has evolved into a game of who has it better—me or you? This type of rivalry can be managed by some and not others. Be mindful it doesn't grow into a friendship roadblock.

They don't respect it when you say no. Respect for boundaries is a crucial component of healthy friendships. In healthy friendships, friends understand that sometimes they will be told no and this is okay.

This list is not exhaustive, as there are other things, such as violence, that indicate an unhealthy relationship and that should not be tolerated. Likewise, the more you get to know someone, the better you can determine if your personalities are a good fit for one another. Saying no to friendship after all of the time you have invested is really, really hard. But sometimes it is better to slow down or end the friendship before it progresses to the point where it is too bad to stay and too good to leave. Although there is not a great deal of research on the impact of unhealthy friendships on one's mental and physical well-being, it's obvious that any unhealthy relationship is not good for anyone.

If you are at a crossroads where you have decided to shed a relationship, have an open, honest, and transparent dialogue with your problematic friend before cutting them out of your life forever. Friendship is important and hard to find, and sometimes the simple act of bringing awareness to the situation can ameliorate conflict and promote attunement between friends. However, if your friend is not able to hear your perspective and is unwilling to change, explain that you need space or just take space without an explanation. While it is obviously preferable and adult-like to discuss your differences, sometimes you can't, and if it is a matter of self-preservation, just keep your distance. Consider the case of Ellie who, when she was single and dating, befriended Joanne. They were thicker than thieves until Ellie started to date a guy seriously. Joanne started to act in inappropriate, jealous ways that nearly sabotaged Ellie's new relationship. Ellie had to make the decision that Joanne's behavior was too threatening and toxic for her life and simply had to pull away. Ellie never felt good about not getting to confront Joanne, but after careful consideration decided that this was the best thing for her.

Summary

Life would be so much easier if, after the act of finding and making friends, you could just have a group of besties forever. However, this is not the case, and friendship will always require work. Friendship is about camaraderie, companionship, and love. If you have friendships where these three characteristics are blossoming, maintaining them is a joy and a pleasure in and of itself. Ending friendships is sometimes necessary and painful. However, It is important to love and honor yourself first, even if it means letting go of someone who knows and cares about you. By cutting out the people in your life who are undeserving of you, you are creating more space for those who are truly deserving of you!

CONCLUSION

We have come to the end of your journey to find, make, and keep friends. You have done the work to get to this point, and you can continue to use these tools, strategies, mantras, and case examples along your way. While there are several things that you may take from this book, the one hope I have is that you start to see yourself as the good friend that you are, and that you are worthy of having friends that love and care for you. Loving yourself and seeing your own value is a natural aphrodisiac—we know the clichéd saying that the more you love yourself, the more others will love you. It is the truth and a justifiably overused saying.

Friendship can provide endless opportunities for fun, laughter, and companionship, as well as offer some incredibly painful and stinging moments. These moments will happen. You will be rejected and pained deeply by friendships that you wanted to last forever. Know that, even though it may feel like it is about you, most of the time it is not. We are all humans who come with our own baggage—sometimes our baggage can be comingled and sometimes we each need our own suitcases. Sometimes friendships that you thought were over will take a 20-year hiatus and a newer, better friendship will blossom. As is reflected by the famous Thich Nhat Hanh, *"No mud, no lotus."* It takes hard work to have friendships, but with time and effort it will be worth it.

Finally, I wish you the best of luck on the road ahead, wherever it may take you. I hope that you practice gratitude for the friendships you do have and, if you are struggling, can more deeply appreciate the friendships you are about to find once you put down this book.

APPENDIX

This appendix lists resources for meeting new people. This list is not exhaustive but is a good starting point. Please note that not all the suggestions listed below are appropriate for everyone.

In-Person Groups

Alcoholics Anonymous. Every location has regular meetings, and it is widely known for their community and community-building efforts.

Art meet-ups. Many local galleries have opening nights for new artists and, typically, they are open to the public.

Book clubs. Check out your local library or bookstore.

Beer/wine tours. Many breweries and wine stores host regular tastings or tours.

Hiking clubs. Outdoor outfitters often organize hiking events. Check out stores like REI.

Professional affinity/work networking events. These opportunities are not only good for expanding your professional opportunities, but also give you the space to practice socializing with new people who have a shared interest.

Toastmasters. Public speaking forum for those who struggle with public speaking.

Volunteer opportunities. Consider your local hospital, human services agency, shelter, or after-school program. VolunteerMatch.org is a great way to get connected to events in your community.

BIBLIOGRAPHY

Ader, Jason. *Friendship in Aristotle's Nicomachean Ethics.* Parkland College, 2011. https://spark.parkland.edu/cgi/viewcontent.cgi?article=1038&context=ah.

Ainsworth, Mary D. Salter, Mary Blehar, Everett Waters, and Sally N. Wall. *Patterns of Attachment: A Psychological Study of the Strange Situation.* New York: Routledge, Taylor & Francis Group, 2015.

Benenson, Joyce F. and Athena Christakos. "The Greater Fragility of Females' Versus Males' Closest Same-Sex Friendships." *Child Development* 74, no. 4 (2003): 1123–129. https://doi.org/10.1111/1467-8624.00596.

Berndt, Thomas J., Jacquelyn A. Hawkins, and Ziyi Jiao. "Influences of Friends and Friendships on Adjustment to Junior High School." *Merrill-Palmer Quarterly* 45, no. 1 (November 30, 1998): 13–41. https://eric.ed.gov/?id=EJ582404.

Berndt, Thomas J. "Friendship Quality and Social Development." *Current Directions in Psychological Science* 11, no. 1 (2002): 7–10. doi:10.1111/1467-8721.00157.

Bhattacharya, Kunal, Asim Ghosh, Daniel Monsivais, et al. "Sex Differences in Social Focus across the Life Cycle in Humans." *Royal

HERE TO MAKE FRIENDS

Society Open Science 3, no. 4 (2016): 160097. https://doi.org/10.1098/
rsos.160097.

Bonior, Andrea. *The Friendship Fix: The Complete Guide to Choosing,
Losing, and Keeping up with Your Friends.* New York: Thomas Dunne
Books, 2011.

Brown, Brené. *Daring Greatly: How the Courage to Be Vulnerable
Transforms the Way We Live, Love, Parent, and Lead.* London: Penguin
Life, 2015.

Byrne, Rhonda. *The Secret.* New York: Atria Books, 2018.

Cable, Noriko, Mel Bartley, Tarani Chandola, et al. "Friends Are
Equally Important to Men and Women, but Family Matters More for
Men's Well-being." *Journal of Epidemiology and Community Health* 67,
no. 2 (2012): 166–71. https://doi.org/10.1136/jech-2012-201113.

CBS News. "Many Americans Are Lonely, and Gen Z Most of All,
Study Finds." May 4, 2018. https://www.cbsnews.com/news/
many-americans-are-lonely-and-gen-z-most-of-all-study-finds.

Cigna, a Global Health Insurance and Health Service Company.
"New Cigna Study Reveals Loneliness at Epidemic Levels in America."
Accessed May 11, 2019. https://www.cigna.com/newsroom/news-
releases/2018/new-cigna-study-reveals-loneliness-at-epidemic-levels
-in-america.

Crosnoe, Robert. "Friendships in Childhood and Adolescence: The
Life Course and New Directions." *Social Psychology Quarterly* 63, no. 4
(2000): 377. https://doi.org/10.2307/2695847.

Dunbar, R. I. M. "The Anatomy of Friendship." *Trends in Cognitive
Sciences* 22, no. 1 (January 2018): 32–51. https://doi.org/10.1016/j.tics.2017
.10.004.

Ferrazzi, Keith. "Connecting with Connectors." Inc.com. March 01,
2005. https://www.inc.com/resources/sales/articles/20050301/
connections.html.

Fottrell, Quentin. "People Spend Most of Their Waking Hours Staring at Screens." MarketWatch. August 04, 2018. https://www.market watch.com/story/people-are-spending-most-of-their-waking -hours-staring-at-screens-2018-08-01.

Gervis, Zoya. "Why the Average American Hasn't Made a New Friend in 5 Years." *New York Post*. May 10, 2019. https://nypost.com/2019/05/09/ why-the-average-american-hasnt-made-a-new-friend-in-5-years.

Geyer, Peter. "Extraversion-Introversion: What C. G. Jung Meant and How Contemporaries Responded." *Conference Paper: AUSApt National Conference*, October 2012.

Gillath, Omri and Gery Karantzas. "Attachment Security Priming: A Systematic Review." *Current Opinion in Psychology* 25 (February 2019): 86–95. https://www.sciencedirect.com/science/article/pii/ S2352250X1830037X.

Gillath, Omri, Gery Karantzas, and Juwon Lee. "Attachment and Social Networks." *Current Opinion in Psychology* 25 (February 2019): 21–25.

Gillath, Omri, Emre Selcuk, and Phillip R. Shaver. "Moving Toward a Secure Attachment Style: Can Repeated Security Priming Help?" *Social and Personality Psychology Compass* 2, no. 4 (2008): 1651–666. doi:10.1111/j.1751-9004.2008.00120.x.

Gladwell, Malcolm. *The Tipping Point: How Little Things Can Make a Big Difference*. London: Abacus, 2015.

Goldstein, Elisha. *Uncovering Happiness: Overcoming Depression with Mindfulness and Self-Compassion*. New York: Atria Books, 2015.

Gonçalves, Bruno, Nicola Perra, and Alessandro Vespignani. "Modeling Users' Activity on Twitter Networks: Validation of Dunbar's Number." *PLoS ONE* 6, no. 8 (2011). https://doi.org/10.1371/ journal.pone.0022656.

Greif, Geoffrey L. *Buddy System: Understanding Male Friendships*. New York: Oxford University Press, 2009.

Grus, Catherine L. "Relational and Physical Victimization within Friendships: Nobody Told Me There'd Be Friends like These." *Journal of Developmental & Behavioral Pediatrics* 24, no. 2 (2003): 137. https://doi.org/10.1097/00004703-200304000-00028.

Guo, Yuan. "The Influence of Social Support on the Prosocial Behavior of College Students: The Mediating Effect Based on Interpersonal Trust." *English Language Teaching* 10, no. 12 (2017): 158. https://doi.org/10.5539/elt.v10n12p158.

Guralnick, Michael J., Robert T. Connor, Mary A. Hammond, et al. "The Peer Relations of Preschool Children with Communication Disorders." *Child Development* 67, no. 2 (1996): 471–89. https://doi.org/10.2307/1131827.

Hall, Jeffrey A. "Sex Differences in Friendship Expectations: A Meta-analysis." *Journal of Social and Personal Relationships* 28, no. 6 (2010): 723-47. https://doi.org/10.1177/0265407510386192.

Hartl, Amy C., Brett Laursen, and Antonius H. N. Cillessen. "A Survival Analysis of Adolescent Friendships: The Downside of Dissimilarity." *Psychological Science* 26, no. 8 (August 2015): 1304–3115. https://www.ncbi.nlm.nih.gov/pmc/articles/PMC4529362.

Hartup, Willard W. and Nan Stevens. "Friendships and Adaptation in the Life Course." *Psychological Bulletin* 121, no. 3 (1997): 355-70. https://doi.org/10.1037//0033-2909.121.3.355.

Hruschka, Daniel J. *Friendship: Development, Ecology, and Evolution of a Relationship*. Berkeley, CA: University of California Press, 2010.

Hughes, Mary Elizabeth, Linda J. Waite, Louise C. Hawkley, et al. "A Short Scale for Measuring Loneliness in Large Surveys: Results from Two Population-Based Studies." *Research on Aging* 26, no. 6 (2004): 655–72. https://www.ncbi.nlm.nih.gov/pmc/articles/PMC2394670.

Johnson, Sue. *Hold Me Tight: Seven Conversations for a Lifetime of Love*. New York: Little, Brown & Company, 2011.

Knowledge Network and Insight Policy Research. "Loneliness Among Older Adults: A National Survey of Adults 45+." Accessed May 10, 2019. https://assets.aarp.org/rgcenter/general/loneliness_2010.pdf.

Laursen, Brett Paul. *Close Friendships in Adolescence*. San Francisco: Jossey-Bass, 1993.

Levine, Amir, and Rachel Heller. *Attached: The New Science of Adult Attachment and How It Can Help You Find—and Keep—Love*. New York: Tarcherperigee, 2012.

Mendelson, M. J. and F. Aboud. "McGill Friendship Questionairre—Friendship Functions." Accessed July 8, 2019. http://www.midss.org/sites/default/files/unpublished_paper.pdf.

MindTools.com. "Golden Rules of Goal Setting: Five Rules to Set Yourself Up for Success." Accessed July 08, 2019. https://www.mindtools.com/pages/article/newHTE_90.htm.

Narr, Rachel K., Joseph P. Allen, Joseph S. Tan, et al. "Close Friendship Strength and Broader Peer Group Desirability as Differential Predictors of Adult Mental Health." *Child Development* 90, no. 1 (2017): 298–313. https://doi.org/10.1111/cdev.12905.

Neff, Kristin. *Self-Compassion: The Proven Power of Being Kind to Yourself*. New York: William Morrow, 2015.

Neff, Kristin. "Self-Compassion Exercise 1: How Would You Treat a Friend?" Accessed July 11, 2019. https://self-compassion.org/exercise-1-treat-friend.

Oehler, M. and E. Psouni. "Partner in Prime? Effects of Repeated Mobile Security Priming on Attachment Security and Perceived Stress in Daily Life." *Attachment and Human Development* 21 no. 6: 638-657, doi: 10.1080/14616734.2018.1517811.

Rawlins, Williams. "Friendships in Later Life." In *LEA's Communication Series. Handbook of Communication and Aging Research*, 273–99. Mahwah, NJ: Lawrence Erlbaum Associates Publishers, 2004.

Roberto, Karen A. and Jean P. Scott. "Friendships of Older Men and Women: Exchange Patterns and Satisfaction." *Psychology and Aging* 1, no. 2 (1986): 103–09. https://doi.org/10.1037/0882-7974.1.2.103.

Rowe, Angela C. and Katherine B. Carnelley. "Preliminary Support for the Use of a Hierarchical Mapping Technique to Examine Attachment Networks." *Personal Relationships* 12, no. 4 (2005): 499–519. https://doi.org/10.1111/j.1475-6811.2005.00128.x.

Saunders, Jessica, Layla Parast, Susan H. Babey, et al. "Exploring the Differences between Pet and Non-pet Owners: Implications for Human-Animal Interaction Research and Policy." *Plos One* 12, no. 6 (2017). https://doi.org/10.1371/journal.pone.0179494.

ScienceDaily. "Half of Your Friends Lost in Seven Years, Social Network Study Finds." May 27, 2009. https://www.sciencedaily.com/releases/2009/05/090527111907.htm.

Self-Compassion.org. "Compassion Exercise 1: How Would You Treat a Friend?" June 10, 2015. Accessed July 11, 2019. https://self-compassion.org/exercise-1-treat-friend.

Sixsmith, Taylor. *Steps to Making Friends: Attachment and Friendship* (2017), Kindle.

Way, Niobe. *Deep Secrets: Boys' Friendships and the Crisis of Connection.* Cambridge, MA: Harvard Press, 2013.

de Wied, Minet, Susan J. T. Branje, and Wim H. J. Meeus. "Empathy and Conflict Resolution in Friendship Relations among Adolescents." *Aggressive Behavior* 33, no. 1 (2007): 48–55. https://doi.org/10.1002/ab.20166.

Yager, Jan. *When Friendship Hurts: How to Deal with Friends Who Betray, Abandon, or Wound You.* Great Britain: Finch Publishing, 2009.

Bibliography

ACKNOWLEDGMENTS

This book and its insights could not have been written without those who have stood by me throughout my journey, and my clients who have allowed me the privilege of being part of their journey.

Thank you to my dearest, oldest friends—Bree Sposato and Molly Nixon—who have helped me overcome my own bouts of social anxiety and awkwardness during those developmental years and have always given me wise and long-standing words of encouragement, no matter how dire the situation.

To those friends who may not be near but are always close to my heart. Caitie Prior, thank you for always being there for me and giving me sound, sage, and real advice. Katie Morrow, thank you for remembering my favorite song and texting me when you hear it. It is heartwarming to know you still think about me—please know that I think about you too! Adrienne Heflich, you are my ride or die and know just what to do to make me feel better. Miriam Denmark, I am forever grateful for your constant support and counsel. Rebecca Feeney, we are new friends, but you have been an amazing source of strength and encouragement for me. I hope our friendship path is very, very long! And to Valeria Love, who is a super-connector and demonstrated true vulnerability by being an adult and asking me to be your friend—you rock! Lastly, a special thanks to Soren Gandrud who has been by my side through some of life's most challenging times.

I also wish to thank Claire Sielaff, Renee Rutledge, and the staff at Ulysses Press for affording me this opportunity and supporting me along the way.

ABOUT THE AUTHOR

Hope Kelaher is a therapist based in New York City. She has extensive training in relational and systemic therapy and received postgraduate training from the Ackerman Institute for the Family. Hope has a degree in public health from Johns Hopkins University and a clinical social work degree from Columbia University. Her passion is helping those struggling with anxiety and depression find healing connections among family and friends. Hope currently lives in Manhattan, where she is always working to make new friendships and strengthen her existing ones. In her spare time, Hope enjoys long walks with her dog, Luna, training for half-marathons, fishing, rowing, and cooking.